COOKING AT A GLANCE

PIES & PASTRIES

FOG CITY PRESS

PUBLISHED BY FOG CITY PRESS
814 MONTGOMERY STREET
SAN FRANCISCO, CA 94133 USA

COPYRIGHT © 1994 WELDON OWEN PTY LTD

CHIEF EXECUTIVE OFFICER JOHN OWEN

PRESIDENT TERRY NEWELL

ART DIRECTOR KYLIE MULQUIN

EDITORIAL MANAGER JANINE FLEW

PRODUCTION MANAGER GILLY BIVEN

PRODUCTION COORDINATOR KYLIE LAWSON

BUSINESS MANAGER EMILY JAHN

VICE PRESIDENT INTERNATIONAL SALES
STUART LAURENCE

PROJECT MANAGING EDITOR TORI RITCHIE

CONTRIBUTING EDITOR JANE HORN

PROJECT DESIGNER PATTY HILL

FOOD PHOTOGRAPHER CHRIS SHORTEN

STEPS PHOTOGRAPHER KEVIN CANDLAND

FOOD STYLISTS SUSAN MASSEY, HEIDI
GINTNER, AND VICKI ROBERTS-RUSSELL

PROP STYLIST LAURA FERGUSON

A CATALOG RECORD FOR THIS BOOK IS
AVAILABLE FROM THE LIBRARY OF CONGRESS,
WASHINGTON, DC.

ISBN 1-892374-49-8

MANUFACTURED BY KYODO PRINTING CO.
(S'PORE) PTE LTD
PRINTED IN SINGAPORE
A WELDON OWEN PRODUCTION

Cover Recipe: Caramel-Apple Pie, page 54
Opposite Page: Apple Butter-Pumpkin Pie,
page 28

CONTENTS

4

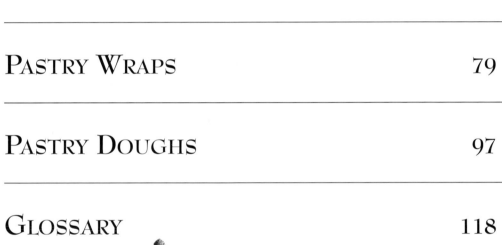

Introduction

YEARS AGO, aspiring home cooks learned to make tender, golden pies and pastries by watching their grandmothers and mothers. Today, our love of pies and pastries hasn't diminished, but few of us have the time or opportunity to learn from a master baker.

That's why Better Homes and Gardens® created this series: to bring into your home our one hundred-plus years of combined kitchen experience. For each book, we've developed sixty new recipes and presented them in a vivid step-by-step format designed to appeal to any cook, from novice to experienced.

If you relish home-baked specialties but believe that a flaky pie crust is an impossible dream, this is the book to turn to for answers. Every important step for making exquisite pies, tarts, dumplings, turnovers, and a wealth of other pastry-based delights is shown in a full-color photograph and explained in clear, easy-to-understand language. It's all there at a glance, as if you were looking over the shoulder of one of our test-kitchen professionals.

An introductory chapter covers the basics of dough preparation. Succeeding chapters focus on a particular type of pastry, from the classic American one- and two-crust pies to elegant European tarts to magnificent puff pastry creations. Each section begins with an overview of essential techniques, then builds on what you have just learned with additional steps, special flourishes, and tempting

Peach Tatin, page 27

recipes. Every chapter is color-coded and every recipe features a "steps at a glance" box that uses these colors to guide you to the photographic steps necessary for its preparation. Valuable tips appear on every page, from basic equipment needs to helpful hints from the experts to stylish yet easy serving ideas. A glossary provides practical information on ingredients used in the book.

On the pages ahead, you'll find sweet and savory examples of the baker's art such as Lemon Angel Pie, Peach Tatin, Chicken-Asparagus Quiche, Plum Dumplings, and Chocolate-Raspberry Napoleons. These and dozens more are beautifully photographed to inspire you. So don't hesitate to get started. You'll be amazed at how easy it is to master pies and pastries *at a glance*.

The Basics

Steps for Making Pie Pastry

BASIC TOOLS FOR MAKING DOUGH

The tools and ingredients that you need
to prepare an all-purpose pastry dough are
very basic; you may already have many of
them on hand.

DRY
MEASURING
CUPS

MEASURING
SPOON

LARGE BOWL

RUBBER SPATULA

SMALL
BOWL

ICING SPATULA

PASTRY
BLENDER

FORK

SPOON

MAKING DOUGH

WHAT DO CLASSIC DESSERTS like summer berry pies, apple dumplings, savory turnovers, and elegant fruit tarts have in common? All can be made with the simple pie pastry presented in detail in this chapter. On the following pages, you'll find everything you need to know to prepare this versatile dough with confidence and complete success. As you progress through the rest of the book, you'll refer back to these fundamentals again and again, but once you've mastered the basic technique, you'll be comfortable with any recipe in this collection that uses Basic Pie Pastry (recipe on page 14) as its foundation.

Regardless of the form it takes, whether pie, tart, dumpling or turnover, pie pastry begins with a simple dough made from just a few ingredients: flour, fat, and liquid. Shortening is a popular choice for this type of pastry because it produces the flakiest result, although it adds no flavor of its own. Butter has a delicate taste that some bakers prefer, but it makes the crust more firm-textured. The addition of liquid not only binds the mixture, it also contributes moisture that converts to steam in the oven, helping to create flaky layers.

For any pastry dough, accurate measurement ensures consistent, foolproof results. Use dry measuring cups for flour, shortening, and butter not already packaged in premeasured sticks (soften first to room temperature, then rechill before using in pastry). For liquids, use a cup with a lip, a comfortable handle, and markings that are easy to read. To measure, fill the cup, set it on a flat surface, and check at eye level. When using a measuring spoon, fill just to its rim. Blend the ingredients either by hand or in a food processor, as shown on the facing page.

to measure shortening or softened butter, pack it into a dry measuring cup, then level it with a spatula or knife

don't use your fingers to blend a dough made with shortening because it will be too sticky to handle

Using a Food Processor

STEP 1 Cutting in Shortening

Cut the shortening or butter into the flour using the metal blade just until the mixture resembles cornmeal, with a few large pieces remaining.

process with a pulsing action so you don't over-mix the dough

STEP 1 Measuring Flour

Before measuring, lighten the flour by stirring it with a spoon or fork. Gently spoon the flour into a dry measuring cup (don't pack down). Level off the top by sweeping across the rim with a metal icing spatula or the straight edge of a knife.

STEP 2 Cutting in Shortening

With a pastry blender, fork, or two knives, cut in the shortening or butter until the pieces are the size of small peas. Use a light touch; if the mixture is overworked, the crust won't be flaky.

9

STEP 2 Incorporating Liquid

With the machine on, add the water. Stop just when all the water is added (do not allow the dough to form a ball).

be sure the water is very cold; if your tap water isn't cold enough, add ice

to pick up any crumbs, push the ball of dough against the bottom and sides of the bowl

as the water is mixed in, check the texture of the dough, being careful not to touch the blade

STEP 3 Incorporating Water

Sprinkle water, 1 tablespoon at a time, over part of the flour and shortening or butter mixture, while gently tossing with a fork to combine. Push moistened dough to one side of the bowl; repeat until all the dough is moistened (you may not use all of the water).

STEP 4 Forming into a Ball

After the shortening or butter, water, and dry ingredients are combined, gather the dough into a ball by scooping up and compressing the mixture with your hands or by pulling it together with a fork.

Steps for Making Pie Pastry

BASIC TOOLS FOR ROLLING AND TRANSFERRING
A sturdy rolling pin, heat-resistant glass pie plate, and pastry brush with firmly attached bristles will provide years of good use in pie making.

ROLLING PIN

PASTRY BRUSH

9-INCH PIE PLATE

ROLLING AND TRANSFERRING DOUGH

ONCE THE SHORTENING or butter, and water have been combined, the next steps in making pastry are to roll the dough into a thin, even disc and to gently fit it into a pie plate or pan.

A variety of sufaces work well for rolling out dough; use the one most easily available to you. A smooth countertop provides the largest work area, while a wooden or plastic board has the advantage of portability and can be stored when not in use. Marble is a good choice because it stays cool (a plus when working with dough), but it is heavy and expensive.

Choose a rolling pin that feels comfortable and rotates smoothly. Generously flour both rolling pin and work surface — as well as the dough — to prevent sticking. Excess flour is easily swept away with a pastry brush later on. Or, slip a cloth stocking over the pin (be aware, though, that the ribbing imprints the dough) and work on a flour-sprinkled pastry cloth.

For an evenly browned pie, select a heat-resistant glass or dull metal pie plate. Dark metal pans cause crusts to brown faster and darker, while shiny metal deflects heat and is best reserved for unbaked crumb crusts. Ceramic is the least effective heat conductor.

before flattening, sprinkle the work surface generously with flour and spread the flour out evenly with a rolling pin

STEP 1 FLATTENING DOUGH
Set the ball of dough on a floured surface. Prepare the dough for rolling by flattening it into a thick, round disc. Press down while at the same time patting the edges to keep them smooth and in a circle.

10

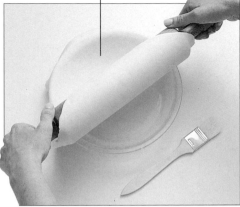

always roll from the center just to the edge of the dough without going off the sides of the pastry

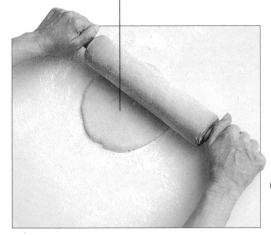

STEP 2 ROLLING DOUGH

Dust the surface with more flour, if needed, and rub the rolling pin with flour. With a light, fluid movement, roll from the center of the dough out to the edges. Move the rolling pin around the dough to make a circle that is uniformly thick and well shaped. Alternatively, roll the dough, give it a quarter turn, then roll again. Repeat this rolling and turning action until the dough is of the desired thickness.

if necessary, brush excess flour from the dough with a pastry brush

STEP 3 TRANSFERRING DOUGH

Loosely drape the dough around the rolling pin and lay it across the pie plate. Unroll and gently ease the dough into the plate without stretching it.

if the dough cracks when unfolded, gently press the trouble spots together to seal

STEP 4 TRANSFERRING BY HAND

If you prefer, fold the dough in half, then in half again, and set it in the pie plate, placing the center point in the middle of the plate. Carefully unfold. Be sure to center the dough so there is an even amount around the edge.

11

An evenly rolled, untrimmed pie crust is the first step in successful pie making.

Steps for Making Pie Pastry

ALUMINUM FOIL

Aluminum foil, scissors, and a fork are handy kitchen implements for trimming and baking pie pastry.

FORK

KITCHEN SCISSORS

12

TRIMMING AND BAKING

AFTER TRANSFERRING the dough to the pie plate, the overhanging edge must be cut off. When the excess dough is trimmed and turned under, it forms a thick rim that is both decorative and practical. Not only does it frame the pie, it also holds in the filling and adds support should the sides shrink during baking. Like soft clay, pie dough is very responsive. Crimp it, flute it, pinch it into points; the result is edible art. To create beautiful edges, see pages 17 and 18.

Some crusts are either partially or fully baked before filling so they will stay crisp. Crusts for custard or cream pies, for example, are partially baked; crusts for uncooked fresh fruit, a chilled mixture such as mousse, or a cooked pastry cream or citrus curd are fully baked. To make a partially baked shell, weight the crust with heavy-duty aluminum foil to keep it flat during baking. To make a fully baked pastry shell, first prick the crust evenly with a fork so it won't puff up and lose its shape. To prevent the edge of an *unbaked* filled pie from over-browning, cover it during the early stages of baking with a foil shield that you can easily make yourself.

for a two-crust pie, the bottom crust would be trimmed to the pie plate's outer edge after filling (see page 44)

STEP 1   TRIMMING THE BOTTOM CRUST
With sharp kitchen scissors or a knife, trim the dough to ½ inch beyond the edge of the pie plate. Fold the excess under to build up a thick rim for crimping.

set the foil on the pastry and gently fit it in so as not to deform the dough

13

STEP 2 PARTIALLY BAKING A CRUST

If the dough is to be partially baked before it is filled, line it with a double thickness of heavy-duty foil to keep it from puffing up in the oven. Form the foil before you place it in the pie plate, or mold it around another pie plate of the same size.

The edge of this Crumb-topped Apple-Raspberry Pie (page 30) has been trimmed and folded under (but not crimped) for a simple, homey look.

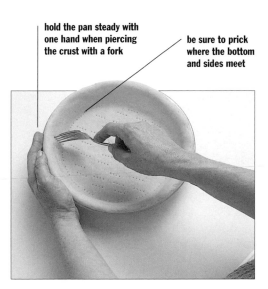

hold the pan steady with one hand when piercing the crust with a fork

be sure to prick where the bottom and sides meet

STEP 3 FULLY BAKING A CRUST

When a crust needs to be fully baked before filling, it must first be pricked all over so that the steam built up during cooking can escape. Then line the crust with a double thickness of foil, as shown in step 2.

STEP 4 PLACING A FOIL SHIELD

Covering the edge of an unbaked, filled pastry shell with aluminum foil during the initial stage of baking will prevent it from overbrowning. To make a shield, fold a 12-inch square of heavy-duty foil in quarters, then cut or tear a quarter circle 3½ inches from the point to make a 7-inch hole. Unfold and place over the pie.

Basic Pie Pastry

Preparation Time: 15 minutes
Chilling Time: 1 to 24 hours (optional)

INGREDIENTS

PASTRY FOR SINGLE-CRUST PIE

1-1/4	CUPS ALL-PURPOSE FLOUR
1/4	TEASPOON SALT
1/3	CUP SHORTENING OR COLD BUTTER
3	TO 4 TABLESPOONS WATER

PASTRY FOR DOUBLE-CRUST PIE

2	CUPS ALL-PURPOSE FLOUR
1/2	TEASPOON SALT
2/3	CUP SHORTENING OR COLD BUTTER
6	TO 7 TABLESPOONS WATER

14

*F*undamental to many recipes throughout this book, this basic pie dough results in a tender, flaky crust every time. Follow the directions on pages 8 through 13 for easy-to-follow details on preparing the dough and rolling, trimming, and baking it.

■ **For pastry for single-crust pie**, in a mixing bowl stir together flour and salt. Cut in shortening or butter till pieces are the size of small peas. Sprinkle *1 tablespoon* of the water over part of the mixture; gently toss with a fork. Push to side of bowl. Repeat till all is moistened (you may not need all of the water). Form dough into a ball. (If desired, chill for 1 to 24 hours.) On a lightly floured surface, flatten dough with hands. Roll dough from center to edges, forming a circle about 12 inches in diameter (or as indicated in recipe). Wrap pastry around rolling pin. Unroll onto a 9-inch pie plate (or as indicated in recipe). Or, fold pastry into quarters and place in pie plate; unfold. Ease pastry into pie plate, being careful not to stretch pastry. Trim to ½ inch beyond edge of pie plate; fold extra pastry under. Crimp edge, if desired. Bake as directed in recipe.

■ **For pastry for double-crust pie**, prepare dough as directed above, *except* divide dough in half. Form each half into a ball. (If desired, chill for 1 to 24 hours.) On a lightly floured surface, flatten one ball of dough with hands. Roll dough from center to edges, forming a circle about 12 inches in diameter (or as indicated in recipe). Wrap pastry around rolling pin. Unroll onto a 9-inch pie plate (or as indicated in recipe). Or, fold pastry into quarters and place in pie plate; unfold. Ease pastry into pie plate, being careful not to stretch pastry. Fill with desired filling. Trim pastry even with rim of pie plate. For top crust, roll remaining dough. Cut slits to allow steam to escape. Place top crust on filling. Trim top crust ½ inch beyond edge of plate. Fold top crust under bottom crust; crimp edge or press together with the tines of a fork. Bake as directed in recipe.

■ **To prepare pastry in a food processor**, place the steel blade in work bowl. Add flour, salt, and shortening or butter. Process with on/off turns till most of the mixture resembles cornmeal but a few larger pieces remain. With machine running, quickly add 3 tablespoons water for single-crust pie, or ¼ cup cold water for double-crust pie, through the feed tube. Stop processor as soon as all water is added. Scrape down sides. Process with 2 on/off turns (mixture may not all be moistened). Remove from bowl and shape into 1 or 2 equal balls. (If desired, chill for 1 to 24 hours.) Continue as above.

■ **For a fully baked pastry shell,** prepare as above, except prick bottom and sides of crust generously with the tines of a fork. Prick where bottom and sides meet all around crust. Line pastry shell with a double thickness of foil. Bake in a preheated 450° oven for 8 minutes. Remove foil and bake for 5 to 6 minutes more or till golden. Cool on a rack.

One-Crust Pies

Steps for Basic Crimping

ROLLING PIN

FORK

9-INCH PIE PLATE

BASIC TOOLS FOR CRIMPING

A rolling pin, pie plate, and fork are necessary for preparing a pie shell, while your hands are the creative tools that you use to make a decorative edge.

16

ONCE THE DOUGH for a one-crust pie has been prepared and shaped as directed on pages 8 through 14, its edge is ready for the finishing touch. Over the years, generations of pie makers have devised decorative patterns for the plain rim of a pie shell. Some of these edges have become traditional favorites and the hallmark of a well-made pie. Instructions for making classic edges are shown on the facing page. They're very impressive, make a superb frame for any filling, and couldn't be easier to accomplish. With a little practice, you can produce them effortlessly and add them proudly to your pastry skills.

The term for this technique is *crimping,* as in to put a bend, pinch, or wave in something soft and responsive. But that is only the dictionary definition. In reality, a beautifully scalloped edge or one pinched into pointy rickracks is more than just dough marked with the impression of your fingers or a tool. It is a work of simple beauty.

The more dough you have to work with, the easier it is to create a pattern. When you roll out the crust, be sure that it will extend beyond the sides of the pie pan. Give yourself at least a ½-inch margin, or even more. After this extra dough is turned under, pinch it gently to pull it up. Then work around the edge of the pie, developing the pattern as evenly as possible.

You'll find examples of finished edges throughout the pages in this chapter and the next. You'll also find slight variations, such as the herringbone hatchmarks on page 35, that will give you ideas to expand your crimping repertoire. On the other hand, allow room for personal expression. Every baker will create an edge that is as individual as a signature.

the width of the scallops (also called flutes) depends on how tightly you press the dough

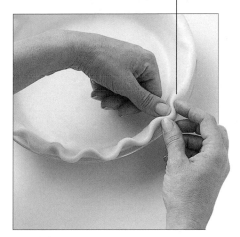

to create an attractive variation, angle and crosshatch the lines into a herringbone pattern

to make a narrow rickrack, set your thumb on its side rather than nail up as shown here

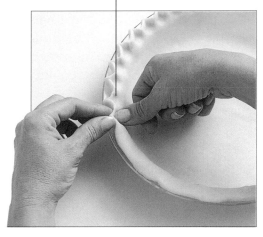

STEP 1 BASIC SCALLOPED EDGE

Place the tip of your thumb against the inside edge of the pie shell. Press the dough around the thumb from the outside edge with the thumb and index finger of your other hand.

STEP 2 FLOWER PETAL EDGE

Make a scalloped edge, with each scallop wide enough to accommodate the tines of a fork. Press down lightly on each outward curve with the fork to create parallel lines.

STEP 3 RICKRACK EDGE

Set your thumb inside the edge of the shell as for a basic scallop. With your other hand, pinch the outside edge to form a point.

17

rotate the pie after each pinch to keep the pattern evenly spaced

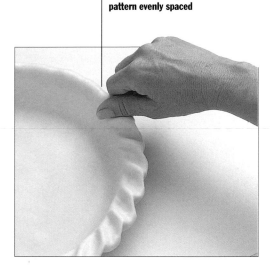

STEP 4 ROPE EDGE

Make the edge as tall and thick as possible. Pinch at an angle with the thumb and bent index finger of one hand; as you pinch, twist forward with the finger and back with the thumb.

This classic rickrack edge will complement any pie filling.

Steps for Making Cutout Edges

CRIMPING IS ONLY one way to dress up the edge of a pie shell. Tiny dough cutouts, secured to the crust with water or an egg wash, are a charming, more elaborate alternative. Standard cookie cutters are too large for this purpose, but hors d'oeuvre or aspic cutters are just the right size. Look for the small cutters, sold in sets, at cookware stores or in mail-order catalogs that specialize in baking. Be sure that they have sharp edges so they will cut the dough cleanly. Match the shape to the occasion or take inspiration from the filling. Try crescent moons and stars for a New Year's Eve chocolate pie, or create a border of leaves for a harvest pie made with tree fruits such as apples or pears. You can also attach leaves and other shapes that have been made freehand, as shown on page 28. To have enough dough for these pastry shapes, you will need to prepare the recipe for a double-crust pie.

18

use leftover dough to make tartlets, or sprinkle with cinnamon-sugar and bake as cookies

STEP 1 MAKING CUTOUTS

Dip a small cutter in flour, then press firmly into the extra rolled-out pastry dough. Cut out shapes as close together as possible.

first trim the dough flush to the rim of the pan (see page 44) to create a flat surface for the cutouts

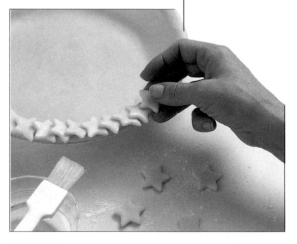

STEP 2 APPLYING CUTOUTS

Lightly brush the edge of the pie with water or a beaten egg. Arrange the pastry shapes on the moistened rim, pressing gently to adhere. Overlap them slightly to build up the edge.

Steps for Making Cookie Crusts

A CRUMB CRUST is wonderfully simple. There isn't any dough to mix or roll out; just crush or grind whole cookies into fine crumbs, bind with butter or margarine, and press into a pie pan. Better still, a crumb crust can usually be made ahead, filled, and chilled. Good choices for crumb crusts include gingersnaps, chocolate or vanilla wafers, and graham crackers.

Change the texture and flavor with additions such as chopped nuts and grated orange peel. For some tempting ways to use a cookie crust, see Peanut Butter Cream Pie with Chocolate Lace, page 23, and Pumpkin Ice Cream Pie, page 39.

19

ROLLING PIN AND
PLASTIC BAG

9-INCH PIE
PLATE

BASIC TOOLS FOR COOKIE CRUSTS

A pie plate is a must for any pie shell, but a cookie crust requires some additional equipment, including a custard cup, a rolling pin, and a heavy-duty plastic bag.

CUSTARD
CUP

leave the end of the bag open slightly so air can escape as you roll

you can use your fingers to press in the crumbs, but they will get sticky

STEP 1 CRUSHING COOKIES BY HAND
Place whole cookies in a large, heavy-duty plastic bag. Roll across the bag with a rolling pin. Repeat until the cookies are crushed to fine crumbs.

STEP 2 CRUSHING IN A PROCESSOR
Or, break the cookies into pieces and place into the work bowl of a food processor. Set the cover in place, then process by pulsing on and off until the cookie pieces are finely ground.

STEP 3 PRESSING INTO THE PAN
With the bottom edge of a custard cup or the back of a spoon, spread and tamp down the crumbs in an even layer over the bottom and sides of the pie pan.

Old-fashioned Butterscotch Pie

INGREDIENTS

FULLY BAKED PASTRY SHELL
(PAGE 14)

FILLING

1-1/2	CUPS PACKED BROWN SUGAR
1/4	CUP ALL-PURPOSE FLOUR
1/8	TEASPOON SALT
3	BEATEN EGG YOLKS
1-1/2	CUPS MILK
2	TABLESPOONS MARGARINE OR BUTTER
1	TEASPOON VANILLA

MERINGUE

3	EGG WHITES
1/4	TEASPOON CREAM OF TARTAR
6	TABLESPOONS SUGAR

If you like the deep, rich taste of brown sugar, use dark brown sugar in this recipe; otherwise, prepare it with light brown sugar for a lighter color and flavor.

■ Prepare and fully bake pastry shell as directed; set aside to cool. For filling, in a heavy, medium saucepan stir together the brown sugar, flour, and salt. Add egg yolks and milk. Cook while stirring with a wire whisk till thickened and bubbly. (Mixture may appear curdled. Stir briskly while cooking and mixture will become smooth.) Cook and stir 2 minutes more. Remove from heat. Stir in margarine or butter and vanilla. Pour hot filling into baked pastry shell.

■ For meringue, in a mixing bowl beat egg whites and cream of tartar with an electric mixer on medium speed about 1 minute, or till soft peaks form (tips curl). Gradually add sugar, 1 tablespoon at a time, beating on high speed about 4 minutes more, or till mixture forms stiff, glossy peaks (tips stand straight) and sugar completely dissolves. Immediately spread meringue over hot filling, spreading to edge of pastry to seal and prevent shrinkage.

■ Bake pie in a preheated 350° oven for 15 minutes. Cool on a rack for 1 hour. Chill 3 to 6 hours before serving. Store in the refrigerator.

Makes 8 servings

Per serving: 422 calories, 6 g protein, 68 g carbohydrate, 14 g total fat (4 g saturated), 83 mg cholesterol, 195 mg sodium, 265 mg potassium

Preparation Time: 40 minutes
Baking Time: 28 to 29 minutes
Cooking Time: 10 minutes
Chilling Time: 3 to 6 hours

STEPS AT A GLANCE	Page
MAKING PIE PASTRY	8–14
BASIC CRIMPING	16
MAKING MERINGUE	20

STEPS FOR MAKING MERINGUE

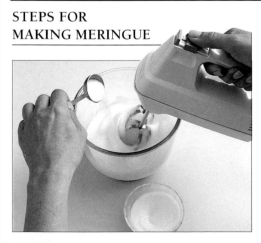

STEP 1 BEATING IN THE SUGAR
Beat the egg whites until the peaks bend over in soft curls when the beaters are lifted from the bowl. Sprinkle in sugar, 1 tablespoon at a time, beating constantly.

STEP 2 TESTING THE PEAKS
The meringue is ready when the egg white–sugar mixture forms glossy peaks that stand up straight when the beaters are removed.

STEP 3 SPREADING ON THE PIE
Spread the meringue with an icing knife or rubber spatula, sealing it completely to the edges. Swirl to make decorative peaks.

An old-fashioned pie server is used to parcel out wedges of this creamy pie. The edge is crimped into a basic scallop.

21

A cool, creamy slice of peanut butter pie is set off by a delicate crown of chocolate lace. The crust is made with pressed-in chocolate wafer crumbs.

22

Peanut Butter Cream Pie with Chocolate Lace

INGREDIENTS

CRUST

1/3	CUP MARGARINE *OR* BUTTER, MELTED
1-1/3	CUPS FINELY CRUSHED CHOCO-LATE WAFERS (ABOUT 25)

FILLING

3/4	CUP WHIPPING CREAM
2	TABLESPOONS SIFTED POWDERED SUGAR
1	TEASPOON VANILLA
1	8-OUNCE PACKAGE CREAM CHEESE, SOFTENED
1/2	CUP PEANUT BUTTER
1/2	CUP SIFTED POWDERED SUGAR
1/4	CUP MILK

CHOCOLATE LACE

1/2	CUP SEMISWEET CHOCOLATE PIECES *OR* CHOPPED SEMISWEET CHOCOLATE
1-1/2	TEASPOONS SHORTENING
1/4	CUP FINELY CHOPPED PEANUTS

*K*ids *of all ages will love this one. For a more informal occasion, skip the lacy chocolate topping and sprinkle the pie with chopped peanuts instead.*

■ For crust, combine margarine or butter and crushed wafers. Spread mixture evenly into a 9-inch pie plate. Press onto bottom and sides to form a firm, even crust. Chill in refrigerator while preparing filling.

■ For filling, in a medium mixing bowl beat whipping cream, 2 tablespoons powdered sugar, and the vanilla till soft peaks form; set aside. In a large mixing bowl beat cream cheese and peanut butter till light and fluffy. Add ½ cup powdered sugar and the milk; beat till smooth and creamy. Fold the whipped cream mixture into the peanut butter mixture. Spoon evenly into the crust. Cover and chill for 4 to 6 hours.

■ For chocolate lace, place the chocolate pieces or chopped chocolate and shortening in a heavy plastic bag. Close bag and put section with chocolate in a small bowl of warm water. Let stand till melted. Snip off one corner of the bag. Pipe small designs onto waxed paper–lined baking sheets. Let stand till dry, then peel the chocolate from the waxed paper and use to garnish each serving. Store in the refrigerator.

Makes 8 servings

Per serving: 546 calories, 10 g protein, 35 g carbohydrate, 42 g total fat (15 g saturated), 65 mg cholesterol, 425 mg sodium, 263 mg potassium

Preparation Time: 45 minutes
Chilling Time: 4 to 6 hours

STEPS FOR MAKING CHOCOLATE LACE

STEP 1 MELTING CHOCOLATE
Put the chocolate pieces and shortening in a heavy plastic bag and push all to one corner. Close the bag by securing with a twist tie just above the chocolate-shortening mixture. Set in a bowl of warm water till melted. Rub the bag to blend contents.

STEP 2 PIPING CHOCOLATE
Hold the bag point up, push back a little of the chocolate, and snip a tiny piece from the corner to create an opening. To use, squeeze the bag gently with one hand and guide it with the other. Pipe out designs onto a waxed paper–lined baking sheet. Let harden, then peel off and use, or cover and chill until ready to serve. Experiment with different designs to find one that suits you best. You can compose letters or numbers, if desired.

Lemon Angel Pie

Preparation Time: 1 hour
Baking Time: 45 minutes
Cooking Time: 10 minutes
Chilling Time: 2 to 24 hours

INGREDIENTS

MERINGUE SHELL

3	EGG WHITES
1	TEASPOON VANILLA
1/4	TEASPOON CREAM OF TARTAR
1	CUP SUGAR

FILLING

1/2	CUP SUGAR
3	TABLESPOONS CORNSTARCH
1-1/3	CUPS MILK
3	BEATEN EGG YOLKS
1/2	CUP DAIRY SOUR CREAM
2	TEASPOONS FINELY SHREDDED LEMON PEEL
1/4	CUP LEMON JUICE

GARNISH

	WHIPPED CREAM (OPTIONAL)
	LEMON PEEL (OPTIONAL)
	RASPBERRIES (OPTIONAL)

*T*he delicate meringue crust will be crisp if the pie is served soon after assembly. If you prefer a softer crust, make the pie a day ahead and store it in the refrigerator.

■ For meringue shell, in a large mixing bowl beat egg whites, vanilla, and cream of tartar with an electric mixer on medium speed till soft peaks form (tips curl). Gradually add sugar, 1 tablespoon at a time, beating on high speed about 7 minutes, or till very stiff peaks form (tips stand straight) and sugar is almost dissolved. Using a spoon or spatula, spread meringue onto bottom and sides of a well-greased 10-inch pie plate, building the sides up to form a shell. Bake in a preheated 300° oven for 45 minutes. Turn off oven. Let dry in oven with door closed for 1 hour (do not open oven door). Cool on a rack.

■ For filling, in a medium saucepan stir together sugar and cornstarch. Stir in milk. Cook and stir over medium heat till thickened and bubbly. Reduce heat; cook and stir for 2 minutes more. Remove from heat. Gradually stir about *half* of the hot mixture into egg yolks. Return all to saucepan and bring to a gentle boil. Reduce heat. Cook and stir for 2 minutes more. Remove from heat. Stir in sour cream, lemon peel, and lemon juice. Pour filling into a bowl. Cover surface with plastic wrap. Cool without stirring. Spoon filling into meringue shell. Cover and chill for 2 to 24 hours.

■ Just before serving, if desired, garnish with dollops of whipped cream, lemon peel, and raspberries.
Makes 8 servings

Per serving: 230 calories, 4 g protein, 42g carbohydrate, 6 g total fat (3 g saturated), 89 mg cholesterol, 52 mg sodium, 122 mg potassium

STEPS AT A GLANCE	Page
MAKING MERINGUE	20
MAKING MERINGUE SHELL	24

24

STEPS FOR MAKING MERINGUE SHELL

STEP 1 SPREADING MERINGUE
With a rubber spatula or spoon, spread the meringue in a greased pie plate. Remove any buildup from the spatula by dipping it in cold water and wiping it clean.

STEP 2 COATING THE SIDES
Be sure that the bottom and sides are uniformly thick. As you build the shell, push up the sides to form a high edge.

25

To make lemon twists, remove peel with a zesting tool, then poach it lightly in a sugar syrup. Or, just sprinkle the pie with grated lemon peel.

Presented on a Provençal platter,
Peach Tatin looks glorious
with a pattern of mint leaves
around the rim.

26

Peach Tatin

*H*ere's *a peachy twist on the classic French apple pastry, tarte tatin. Cook peaches in the caramel sauce, then cover them with pastry and bake. Invert the pie to show off the glazed peaches. Offer with yogurt or sour cream, if desired.*

■ In a 10-inch ovenproof skillet combine ⅔ cup sugar and ½ cup butter. Bring to boiling over medium heat, stirring occasionally. Reduce heat to medium-low and cook, without stirring, for 8 to 10 minutes more, or till mixture just begins to turn brown. (Mixture may separate.) Remove from heat.

■ Arrange peaches, pitted sides up, in a layer on top of the sugar mixture, overlapping if necessary. Cover and cook over low heat about 10 minutes, or till peaches are tender.

■ Meanwhile, in a medium mixing bowl combine the flour and ¼ cup sugar. Cut in ⅔ cup butter till pieces are the size of small peas. Using a fork, stir in egg till all dough is moistened. Form dough into a ball.

■ On a lightly floured surface, slightly flatten dough. Roll dough into a 10-inch circle, trimming to make an even circle. Cut slits in pastry. Wrap pastry around rolling pin; carefully unroll over peaches in skillet. Bake in a preheated 375° oven about 30 minutes, or till pastry is golden. Remove skillet from oven. Cool in skillet on a rack for 5 minutes. Invert onto a large serving plate; lift off skillet. Serve warm with yogurt or sour cream, if desired.

Makes 8 servings

Per serving: 490 calories, 5 g protein, 59 g carbohydrate, 28 g total fat (22 g saturated), 99 mg cholesterol, 322 mg sodium, 304 mg potassium

STEPS AT A GLANCE	Page
MAKING PIE PASTRY	8–11
MAKING PEACH TATIN	27

Preparation Time: 35 minutes
Cooking Time: 18 to 20 minutes
Baking Time: 30 minutes

INGREDIENTS

2/3	CUP SUGAR
1/2	CUP BUTTER
2	POUNDS PEACHES, PEELED, PITTED, AND QUARTERED (6 CUPS)
2	CUPS ALL-PURPOSE FLOUR
1/4	CUP SUGAR
2/3	CUP BUTTER
1	SLIGHTLY BEATEN EGG
1/2	CUP PLAIN YOGURT OR DAIRY SOUR CREAM (OPTIONAL)

27

STEPS FOR MAKING PEACH TATIN

STEP 1 ARRANGING THE PEACHES
After the sugar mixture has dissolved and browned slightly, cover with the peach quarters, arranged pitted side up. If necessary, lay the peaches on their sides, overlapping to fit in the skillet.

STEP 2 TRIMMING THE CRUST
Use a 10-inch plate or cake pan as a template. With a small, sharp knife, cut out a circle of dough. Lay the dough over the peaches, but don't let it touch the pan sides or it will stick when turned out.

STEP 3 INVERTING THE PIE
Cool the pie briefly. Place a serving plate larger in diameter than the pie over the skillet, then, holding the bottom of the skillet with a hot pad, invert the skillet and plate so that the pan is on top. Slowly lift off the skillet.

Apple Butter–Pumpkin Pie

A pple butter lends its fruity flavor to this harvest pie. If you have pumpkin pie spice on hand, use 2 teaspoons of it in place of the cinnamon, ginger, and nutmeg called for in the recipe. To make the leaf decoration shown here, prepare pastry for a double-crust pie.

■ In a large mixing bowl combine pumpkin, apple butter, sugar, cinnamon, ginger, and nutmeg. Add eggs; beat lightly with a rotary beater or wire whisk till combined. Gradually stir in evaporated milk and milk; mix well.

■ Prepare and roll out pastry as directed. Line a 9-inch pie plate with pastry. Trim and crimp a high pastry edge or attach leaf-shaped cutouts. Pour pumpkin mixture into pastry shell. To prevent overbrowning, cover edge of pie with foil. Bake in a preheated 375° oven for 25 minutes. Remove foil and bake about 25 minutes more, or till a knife inserted near center comes out clean. Cool on a rack for 1 hour. Chill 3 to 6 hours before serving. Store in the refrigerator. If desired, serve with whipped cream.

Makes 8 servings

Per serving: 317 calories, 6 g protein, 45 g carbohydrate, 13 g total fat (4 g saturated), 86 mg cholesterol, 119 mg sodium, 286 mg potassium

28

INGREDIENTS

1	CUP CANNED PUMPKIN
1	CUP APPLE BUTTER
1/3	CUP SUGAR
1	TEASPOON GROUND CINNAMON
1/2	TEASPOON GROUND GINGER
1/2	TEASPOON GROUND NUTMEG
3	EGGS
1	5-OUNCE CAN EVAPORATED MILK (2/3 CUP)
1/2	CUP MILK
	PASTRY FOR SINGLE-CRUST *OR* DOUBLE-CRUST PIE, PAGE 14 (SEE RECIPE INTRODUCTION)
	WHIPPED CREAM (OPTIONAL)

Preparation Time: 25 minutes
Baking Time: 50 minutes
Chilling Time: 3 to 6 hours

STEPS AT A GLANCE	Page
MAKING PIE PASTRY	8–14
APPLYING CUTOUTS	18

Attach cut-out pastry leaves for an autumnal edge. Bake the center decoration on a cookie sheet lined with parchment paper in the same oven as the pie for about 15 minutes, then place on top of the cooked pie.

Spiced Pear Pie with Almond Streusel

You can enrich each serving of this fruity dessert with a scoop of whipped cream that has a bit of ground cinnamon stirred into it. Try a flower petal edge (page 17) for the crust.

Preparation Time: 45 minutes
Baking Time: 45 to 50 minutes

INGREDIENTS

PIE

1/3	CUP PACKED BROWN SUGAR
1/3	CUP GRANULATED SUGAR
1/4	CUP ALL-PURPOSE FLOUR
1/2	TEASPOON GROUND CINNAMON
1/2	TEASPOON GROUND NUTMEG
1/4	TEASPOON GROUND GINGER
1/4	TEASPOON GROUND ALLSPICE
6	CUPS SLICED PEELED PEARS (ABOUT 2 POUNDS)
	PASTRY FOR SINGLE-CRUST PIE (PAGE 14)

STREUSEL

3/4	CUP FINELY CRUSHED VANILLA WAFERS (ABOUT 20 WAFERS)
1/2	CUP CHOPPED ALMONDS
3	TABLESPOONS MARGARINE *OR* BUTTER

29

*M*ost baked fruit pies have an upper crust to hold in moisture during cooking; some, like this one, are topped with crumbs that serve the same purpose, but also add extra flavor and crunch.

■ For pie, in a large mixing bowl stir together brown sugar, granulated sugar, flour, cinnamon, nutmeg, ginger, and allspice. Add pears; toss and set aside. Prepare and roll out pastry as directed. Line a 9-inch pie plate with pastry. Trim and crimp edge of pastry. Pour pear mixture into pastry shell.

■ For streusel, in a medium bowl combine crushed vanilla wafers and almonds. Cut in margarine or butter till crumbly. Sprinkle streusel over pie. To prevent overbrowning, cover edge of pie with foil. Bake in a preheated 375° oven for 25 minutes. Remove foil and bake for 20 to 25 minutes more, or till top is golden.

Makes 8 servings

Per serving: 440 calories, 5 g protein, 65 g carbohydrate, 19 g total fat (4 g saturated), 6 mg cholesterol, 147 mg sodium, 313 mg potassium

STEPS AT A GLANCE	Page
MAKING PIE PASTRY	8–14
BASIC CRIMPING	16

Crumb-topped Apple-Raspberry Pie

Preparation Time: 45 minutes
Baking Time: 45 to 60 minutes

INGREDIENTS

PIE

1/2	TO 2/3 CUP SUGAR
1/4	CUP ALL-PURPOSE FLOUR
1/2	TEASPOON GROUND CINNAMON
5	CUPS THINLY SLICED PEELED COOKING APPLES (ABOUT 2 POUNDS)
	PASTRY FOR SINGLE-CRUST PIE (PAGE 14)
2	CUPS FRESH *OR* LOOSE-PACK FROZEN RED RASPBERRIES

TOPPING

1/2	CUP ALL-PURPOSE FLOUR
1/2	CUP PACKED BROWN SUGAR
1/2	TEASPOON GROUND CINNAMON
1/4	TEASPOON GROUND NUTMEG
1/4	CUP MARGARINE *OR* BUTTER
1/4	CUP CHOPPED PECANS *OR* WALNUTS

*H*ere's the perfect way to extend precious raspberries: In this pie, a red ribbon of delectable raspberries rests between two layers of apples, the quintessential pie fruit. A crumbly, nutty topping finishes it off.

■ For pie, in a large mixing bowl stir together sugar, flour, and cinnamon. Add apples, tossing to coat. Set aside. Prepare and roll out pastry as directed. Line a 9-inch pie plate with pastry. Trim and crimp edge of pastry. Transfer *half* of the apple mixture to pastry shell. Sprinkle with raspberries; add remaining apple mixture.

■ For topping, in a medium mixing bowl stir together flour, brown sugar, cinnamon, and nutmeg. Cut in margarine or butter till crumbly. Stir in pecans or walnuts. Sprinkle topping over pie. To prevent overbrowning, cover edge of pie with foil. Bake in a preheated 375° oven for 25 minutes. Remove foil and bake for 20 to 25 minutes more (30 to 35 minutes if using frozen berries), or till top is golden and edges are bubbly. Cool on a rack.

Makes 8 servings

Per serving: 400 calories, 4 g protein, 60 g carbohydrate, 17 g total fat (3 g saturated), 0 mg cholesterol, 139 mg sodium, 199 mg potassium

With its symmetrical pointed arches, a rickrack edge is a nice counterpoint to a crumbly streusel topping.

30

Sour Cream & Raisin Pie with Meringue

Preparation Time: 30 minutes
Baking Time: 55 to 60 minutes
Chilling Time: 3 to 6 hours

INGREDIENTS

PIE

1	CUP RAISINS
3	EGG YOLKS
1-1/2	CUPS DAIRY SOUR CREAM
1	CUP SUGAR
1/2	CUP MILK
3	TABLESPOONS ALL-PURPOSE FLOUR
1	TEASPOON GROUND CINNAMON
1/4	TEASPOON GROUND NUTMEG
1/4	TEASPOON GROUND CLOVES
	PASTRY FOR SINGLE-CRUST PIE (PAGE 14)
1	TEASPOON GROUND CINNAMON

MERINGUE

3	EGG WHITES
1/2	TEASPOON VANILLA
1/4	TEASPOON CREAM OF TARTAR
6	TABLESPOONS SUGAR

31

For a clever way to trim the crust, cut diamonds of pastry with a fluted wheel and attach like cutouts (page 18).

*C*reate a decorative meringue topping by piping strips of the meringue through a pastry bag fitted with a ½-inch star tip.

■ For pie, in a small saucepan add enough water to raisins to cover. Bring to boiling. Remove from heat. Cover and let stand 5 minutes. Drain raisins; set aside. In a medium mixing bowl use a rotary beater or wire whisk to lightly beat egg yolks just till mixed. Stir in sour cream, sugar, milk, flour, 1 teaspoon cinnamon, the nutmeg, cloves, and raisins. Set aside. Prepare pastry as directed, *except* stir in 1 teaspoon cinnamon with the flour and salt. Roll out and line a 9-inch pie plate with pastry. Trim and crimp edge of pastry, or attach cutouts. Pour raisin mixture into pastry shell. To prevent overbrowning, cover edge of pie with foil. Bake in a preheated 375° oven for 20 minutes. Remove foil and bake 20 to 25 minutes more, or till center appears nearly set when shaken. Remove pie and reduce oven temperature to 350°.

■ For meringue, in a mixing bowl combine egg whites, vanilla, and cream of tartar. Beat with an electric mixer on medium speed about 1 minute, or till soft peaks form (tips curl). Gradually add the sugar, 1 tablespoon at a time, beating on high speed about 4 minutes more, or till mixture forms stiff, glossy peaks (tips stand straight) and sugar completely dissolves. Immediately spread meringue over hot pie filling, carefully spreading to edge of pastry to seal and prevent shrinkage. Bake in the 350° oven for 15 minutes. Cool on a rack for 1 hour. Chill 3 to 6 hours before serving. Store in the refrigerator.

Makes 8 servings

Per serving: 468 calories, 7 g protein, 68 g carbohydrate, 20 g total fat (9 g saturated), 100 mg cholesterol, 124 mg sodium, 275 mg potassium

Sweet Potato Pie with Macadamia Crunch

*T*he past and present come together in this outstanding dessert by merging old-fashioned sweet potato pie with recently popular macadamia nuts. If desired, substitute 1 ½ cups mashed canned sweet potatoes for the cooked fresh sweet potatoes.

■ For pie, peel sweet potatoes. Cut off woody portions and ends. Cut into quarters. Cook, covered, in enough boiling water to cover for 25 to 30 minutes, or till tender; drain and mash. (You should have 1½ cups.) Add margarine or butter to hot potatoes, stirring till melted. Stir in brown sugar, cinnamon, vanilla, ginger, and nutmeg. Stir in eggs and half-and-half or light cream. Set aside. Prepare and roll out pastry as directed. Line a 9-inch pie plate with pastry. Trim and crimp edge of pastry. Pour sweet potato mixture into pastry shell. To prevent overbrowning, cover edge of pie with foil. Bake in a preheated 375° oven for 30 minutes.

■ Meanwhile, for topping, in a small saucepan combine brown sugar, corn syrup, and margarine or butter. Bring to boiling over low heat; simmer for 2 minutes. Remove from heat and stir in vanilla.

■ Remove foil from pie. Sprinkle macadamia nuts or almonds evenly over pie; drizzle with brown sugar–corn syrup mixture. Bake for 20 to 25 minutes more, or till a knife inserted near center comes out clean. Cool on a rack. Store in the refrigerator.

Makes 8 servings

Per serving: 501 calories, 7 g protein, 52 g carbohydrate, 30 g total fat (7 g saturated), 89 mg cholesterol, 204 mg sodium, 349 mg potassium

STEPS AT A GLANCE	Page
MAKING PIE PASTRY	8–14
BASIC CRIMPING	16

Preparation Time: 30 minutes
Cooking Time: 27 to 32 minutes
Baking Time: 50 to 55 minutes

INGREDIENTS

PIE

1	POUND SWEET POTATOES
1/4	CUP MARGARINE *OR* BUTTER, CUT UP
1/2	CUP PACKED BROWN SUGAR
1	TEASPOON GROUND CINNAMON
1	TEASPOON VANILLA
1/2	TEASPOON GROUND GINGER
1/2	TEASPOON GROUND NUTMEG
3	SLIGHTLY BEATEN EGGS
1	CUP HALF-AND-HALF *OR* LIGHT CREAM
	PASTRY FOR SINGLE-CRUST PIE (PAGE 14)

TOPPING

3	TABLESPOONS BROWN SUGAR
3	TABLESPOONS LIGHT CORN SYRUP
1	TABLESPOON MARGARINE *OR* BUTTER
1/2	TEASPOON VANILLA
1	3-1/2-OUNCE JAR MACADAMIA NUTS, CHOPPED, *OR* 3/4 CUP SLICED ALMONDS

A shower of chopped macadamias puts crunch into this traditional Southern pie. For a different flavor, use sliced almonds.

Pecan–Chocolate Chip Pie

To decorate the crust as seen here, build up a high edge and create a loose rickrack crimp, making the points fairly tight.

Preparation Time: 35 minutes
Baking Time: 45 to 50 minutes

INGREDIENTS

3	EGGS
1	CUP LIGHT CORN SYRUP
1/2	CUP SUGAR
1/3	CUP MARGARINE OR BUTTER, MELTED
1	6-OUNCE PACKAGE SEMISWEET CHOCOLATE PIECES (1 CUP) OR 1 CUP CHOPPED SEMISWEET CHOCOLATE
1	CUP PECAN HALVES
	PASTRY FOR SINGLE-CRUST PIE (PAGE 14)
10	PECAN HALVES
1	CUP WHIPPING CREAM, WHIPPED

33

*T*here's only one way to improve on a pecan pie: Add chocolate! The resulting pie is rich and filling, so cut the pieces small.

■ In a medium mixing bowl use a rotary beater or wire whisk to lightly beat eggs just till mixed. Stir in corn syrup, sugar, and melted margarine or butter. Mix well. Reserve 2 *tablespoons* of the chocolate pieces; stir remaining chocolate pieces and 1 cup pecan halves into filling. Set filling aside.

■ Prepare and roll out pastry as directed. Line a 9-inch pie plate with pastry. Trim and crimp edge of pastry. Pour filling into pastry shell. To prevent overbrowning, cover the edge of the pie with foil. Bake in a preheated 350° oven for 25 minutes. Remove foil and bake for 20 to 25 minutes more, or till center appears nearly set when shaken. Cool on a rack.

■ Meanwhile, in a small saucepan melt reserved chocolate pieces over low heat. Dip one end of each of the 10 pecan halves into melted chocolate. Place on a waxed paper–lined baking sheet and refrigerate about 15 minutes, or till chocolate is firm.

■ To serve, dollop whipped cream on each slice. Insert a chocolate-dipped pecan half in each dollop of whipped cream. Store in the refrigerator.

Makes 10 servings

Per serving: 573 calories, 6 g protein, 59 g carbohydrate, 37 g total fat (10 g saturated), 97 mg cholesterol, 176 mg sodium, 162 mg potassium

STEPS AT A GLANCE	Page
MAKING PIE PASTRY	8–14
BASIC CRIMPING	16

Chocolate-Banana Cream Pie

*S*ave *a step in preparing this all-American favorite by substituting ½ cup semisweet chocolate pieces for the chopped chocolate. If you like, sprinkle a handful of peanuts over the bananas for the taste of a banana split.*

■ Prepare and bake pastry shell as directed; set aside. For filling, in a heavy medium saucepan stir together the sugar and flour. Gradually stir in milk. Add chocolate. Cook and stir over medium heat till mixture is thickened and bubbly. Reduce heat. Cook and stir for 2 minutes more. Remove from heat.

■ Gradually stir about *1 cup* of the hot mixture into the beaten egg yolks. Return all to saucepan. Bring to a gentle boil. Cook and stir for 2 minutes more. Remove from heat. Stir in margarine or butter, vanilla and, if desired, almond extract. Arrange banana slices over bottom of baked pastry shell; pour hot filling over banana slices.

■ For meringue, in a mixing bowl combine egg whites, vanilla, and cream of tartar. Beat with an electric mixer on medium speed about 1 minute, or till soft peaks form (tips curl). Gradually add the sugar, 1 tablespoon at a time, beating on high speed about 4 minutes more or till mixture forms stiff, glossy peaks (tips stand straight) and sugar completely dissolves. Immediately spread meringue over hot pie filling, carefully spreading to edge of pastry to seal and prevent shrinkage. Bake in a preheated 350° oven for 15 minutes. Cool on a rack for 1 hour. Chill for 3 to 6 hours before serving. Store in refrigerator.

Makes 8 servings

Per serving: 476 calories, 10 g protein, 72 g carbohydrate, 18 g total fat (7 g saturated), 113 mg cholesterol, 162 mg sodium, 416 mg potassium

34

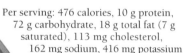

STEPS AT A GLANCE	Page
MAKING PIE PASTRY	8–14
BASIC CRIMPING	16
MAKING MERINGUE	20

Preparation Time: 35 minutes
Baking Time: 38 to 39 minutes
Cooking Time: 12 minutes
Chilling Time: 3 to 6 hours

INGREDIENTS

FULLY BAKED PASTRY SHELL (PAGE 14)

FILLING

3/4	CUP SUGAR
1/2	CUP ALL-PURPOSE FLOUR
3	CUPS MILK
3	OUNCES SEMISWEET CHOCOLATE, CHOPPED
4	BEATEN EGG YOLKS
1	TABLESPOON MARGARINE *OR* BUTTER
1-1/2	TEASPOONS VANILLA
1/4	TO 1/2 TEASPOON ALMOND EXTRACT (OPTIONAL)
3	MEDIUM BANANAS, SLICED (ABOUT 2-1/4 CUPS)

MERINGUE

4	EGG WHITES
1/2	TEASPOON VANILLA
1/4	TEASPOON CREAM OF TARTAR
1/2	CUP SUGAR

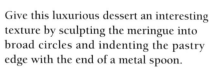

Give this luxurious dessert an interesting texture by sculpting the meringue into broad circles and indenting the pastry edge with the end of a metal spoon.

Chocolate-lined Strawberry Pie

Like chocolate-dipped strawberries, this luscious pie is an extravagant treat. Another time, try making it in a graham cracker or vanilla wafer crust.

■ Prepare and bake pastry shell as directed; set aside to cool. Meanwhile, in a small saucepan melt chocolate pieces and margarine or butter over low heat; set aside. In a heavy saucepan stir together whipping cream and corn syrup. Bring to a gentle boil. Reduce heat and cook 2 minutes. Remove from heat; gradually stir into chocolate mixture. Cool to room temperature. Spread cooled chocolate mixture over the bottom and up the sides of baked pastry shell; set aside.

■ In a blender container or food processor bowl combine *1 cup* of the strawberries and the water. Cover and blend or process till smooth. Add enough additional water to equal 1½ cups liquid. In a medium saucepan combine sugar and cornstarch. Stir in puréed berry mixture. Cook and stir over medium heat till mixture is thickened and bubbly. Cook and stir for 2 minutes more. Cool for 10 minutes without stirring.

■ Arrange *half* of the remaining strawberries, stem end down, in pastry shell. Carefully spoon *half* of the thickened mixture over fruit, thoroughly covering each piece of fruit. Arrange remaining strawberries over first layer. Spoon remaining thickened mixture over fruit, covering each piece of fruit. Chill for 1 to 2 hours before serving.

Makes 8 servings

Per serving: 331 calories, 3 g protein, 48 g carbohydrate, 15 g total fat (4 g saturated), 10 mg cholesterol, 90 mg sodium, 296 mg potassium

INGREDIENTS

	FULLY BAKED PASTRY SHELL (PAGE 14)
1/3	CUP SEMISWEET CHOCOLATE PIECES *OR* CHOPPED SEMISWEET CHOCOLATE
1	TABLESPOON MARGARINE *OR* BUTTER
1/4	CUP WHIPPING CREAM
1	TEASPOON LIGHT CORN SYRUP
8	CUPS MEDIUM STRAWBERRIES, STEMS REMOVED
2/3	CUP WATER
2/3	CUP SUGAR
2	TABLESPOONS CORNSTARCH

Preparation Time: 40 minutes
Baking Time: 13 to 14 minutes
Cooking time: 10 minutes
Chilling Time: 1 to 2 hours

STEPS AT A GLANCE	Page
MAKING PIE PASTRY	8–14
BASIC CRIMPING	16

To make herringbone hatch marks in the crust as shown, press the tines of a fork at alternating angles into the dough.

Piña Colada Pie

Preparation Time: 35 minutes
Baking Time: 18 to 24 minutes
Cooking Time: 10 minutes
Chilling Time: 3 to 6 hours

STEPS AT A GLANCE	Page
MAKING PIE PASTRY	8–14
BASIC CRIMPING	16

INGREDIENTS

3/4	CUP SUGAR
1/3	CUP ALL-PURPOSE FLOUR
2-1/4	CUPS MILK
4	BEATEN EGG YOLKS
1	8-1/4–OUNCE CAN CRUSHED PINEAPPLE, WELL DRAINED
3/4	CUP FLAKED COCONUT
3	TABLESPOONS RUM
1	TABLESPOON MARGARINE OR BUTTER
1-1/2	TEASPOONS VANILLA
	FULLY BAKED PASTRY SHELL (PAGE 14)
1/3	CUP FLAKED COCONUT
1	CUP WHIPPING CREAM, WHIPPED

36

Here's a novel crimping idea: Build up a high pastry edge, then push the handle of a fork or spoon into the dough at sharp angles.

*P*ress the pineapple in a colander with the back of a spoon to ensure that it is well drained before adding to the pie. If you prefer, substitute 3 tablespoons of drained pineapple juice for the rum.

■ In a medium saucepan combine sugar and flour. Gradually stir in milk. Cook and stir over medium-high heat till mixture is thickened and bubbly. Reduce heat. Cook and stir for 2 minutes more. Remove from heat.

■ Gradually stir about *1 cup* of the hot mixture into the egg yolks. Return all to saucepan. Bring to a gentle boil. Cook and stir for 2 minutes more. Remove from heat. Stir in pineapple, ¾ cup coconut, the rum, margarine or butter, and vanilla. Pour hot filling into baked pastry shell. Cool on a rack for 1 hour. Chill for 3 to 6 hours before serving.

■ Meanwhile, spread ⅓ cup coconut in a thin layer in a small baking pan. Bake in a pre-heated 350° oven for 5 to 10 minutes or till golden, stirring once or twice. Remove and cool on a rack.

■ Decorate the pie with the whipped cream. Sprinkle the toasted coconut over the whipped cream. Store in the refrigerator.

Makes 8 servings

Per serving: 483 calories, 7 g protein, 49 g carbohydrate, 28 g total fat (14 g saturated), 152 mg cholesterol, 136 mg sodium, 231 mg potassium

Key Lime Pie

A Key lime is smaller and tarter than the supermarket variety. Most are grown in Florida and not widely available elsewhere, but this creamy pie is good made with any type of lime.

Preparation Time: 30 minutes
Baking Time: 50 minutes
Chilling Time: 3 to 6 hours

■ Prepare and roll out pastry as directed. Line a 9-inch pie plate with pastry. Trim and crimp edge of pastry. Bake pastry in a preheated 450° oven for 5 minutes. Reduce oven temperature to 325°. Meanwhile, for filling, in a bowl beat yolks well with a fork. Gradually stir in sweetened condensed milk and lime peel. Add lime juice, water, and, if desired, food coloring; mix well. (Mixture will thicken.) Spoon into hot pastry shell. Bake in the 325° oven for 30 minutes. Remove from oven. Increase oven temperature to 350°.

■ Meanwhile, for meringue, in a mixing bowl combine egg whites, vanilla, and cream of tartar. Beat with an electric mixer on medium speed about 1 minute, or till soft peaks form (tips curl). Gradually add sugar, 1 tablespoon at a time, beating on high speed about 4 minutes more, or till mixture forms stiff, glossy peaks (tips stand straight) and sugar dissolves. Immediately spread meringue over hot pie filling, carefully spreading to edge of pastry to seal and prevent shrinkage. Bake in the 350° oven 15 minutes; cool 1 hour. Chill 3 to 6 hours before serving.

Makes 8 servings

Per serving: 370 calories, 8 g protein, 51 g carbohydrate, 15 g total fat (6 g saturated), 97 mg cholesterol, 157 mg sodium, 248 mg potassium

STEPS AT A GLANCE	Page
MAKING PIE PASTRY	8–14
BASIC CRIMPING	16
MAKING MERINGUE	20

37

INGREDIENTS

PASTRY FOR SINGLE-CRUST PIE
(PAGE 14)

FILLING

3	EGG YOLKS
1	14-1/2-OUNCE CAN SWEETENED CONDENSED MILK
1/2 TO 3/4	TEASPOON FINELY SHREDDED KEY LIME PEEL *OR* 1-1/2 TEASPOONS FINELY SHREDDED REGULAR LIME PEEL
1/3	CUP LIME JUICE (8 TO 10 KEY LIMES *OR* 2 TO 3 REGULAR LIMES)
1/2	CUP WATER
	FEW DROPS GREEN FOOD COLORING (OPTIONAL)

MERINGUE

3	EGG WHITES
1/2	TEASPOON VANILLA
1/4	TEASPOON CREAM OF TARTAR
1/3	CUP SUGAR

To echo the swirls of meringue, indent the pie crust with the handle of a fork or spoon before baking.

Espresso French Silk Pie

Preparation Time: 25 minutes
Baking Time: 13 to 14 minutes
Chilling Time: 5 to 24 hours

STEPS AT A GLANCE	Page
MAKING PIE PASTRY	8–14
BASIC CRIMPING	16

Refrigerated or frozen egg substitute can replace the raw eggs in this recipe. But do not use margarine instead of butter. Only butter will whip to the silken texture that gives this pie its name.

■ Combine the chocolate and coffee crystals in a heavy small saucepan. Heat over very low heat, stirring constantly till the chocolate begins to melt. Remove pan from heat and stir till smooth. Set aside to cool.

■ In a large mixing bowl beat the sugar and butter with an electric mixer on medium speed about 4 minutes or till fluffy. Stir in the melted chocolate mixture and the vanilla. Add the egg product, ¼ cup at a time (or eggs, one at a time), beating on high speed after each addition and scraping the sides of the bowl. Spoon the filling into the baked pastry shell. Cover and chill in the refrigerator for 5 to 24 hours, or till set. If desired, garnish with whipped cream and strawberry fans.

Makes 10 servings

Per serving: 364 calories, 4 g protein, 34 g carbohydrate, 25 g total fat (12 g saturated), 37 mg cholesterol, 220 mg sodium, 148 mg potassium

INGREDIENTS

3	OUNCES UNSWEETENED CHOCOLATE, CHOPPED
2	TO 3 TEASPOONS INSTANT ESPRESSO COFFEE CRYSTALS
1	CUP SUGAR
3/4	CUP BUTTER, SOFTENED
1	TEASPOON VANILLA
3/4	CUP REFRIGERATED *OR* THAWED FROZEN EGG PRODUCT *OR* 3 EGGS
	FULLY BAKED PASTRY SHELL (PAGE 14)
1/2	CUP WHIPPED CREAM (OPTIONAL)
	STRAWBERRY FANS (OPTIONAL)

To make strawberry fans, slice through the whole berry several times without cutting through the top. Press down on the berry gently with the flat of the knife to fan it out slightly.

Pumpkin Ice Cream Pie

STEPS AT A GLANCE	Page
MAKING COOKIE CRUSTS	19

Preparation Time: 35 minutes
Baking Time: 4 minutes
Freezing Time: 3 hours

INGREDIENTS

GINGERSNAP CRUST

1	CUP FINELY CRUSHED GINGER-SNAPS (ABOUT 14 MEDIUM)
1/4	CUP MARGARINE *OR* BUTTER, MELTED
3/4	CUP FINELY CHOPPED PECANS *OR* WALNUTS
1	TEASPOON FINELY SHREDDED ORANGE PEEL

FILLING

1	PINT VANILLA ICE CREAM (2 CUPS)
1	CUP CANNED PUMPKIN
3/4	CUP PACKED BROWN SUGAR
1	TEASPOON PUMPKIN PIE SPICE *OR* GROUND CINNAMON
1	CUP WHIPPING CREAM, WHIPPED

39

Using a different flavor of ice cream will change this pie every time. You might especially enjoy butter-pecan, rum-raisin, or cinnamon ice cream.

■ For gingersnap crust, stir together crushed gingersnaps and melted margarine or butter. Stir in chopped pecans or walnuts and orange peel. Spread mixture evenly into a 9-inch springform pan. Press onto bottom and about 1 inch up the sides to form a firm, even crust. Bake in a pre-heated 375° oven for 4 minutes. Cool completely on a rack.

■ For filling, place ice cream in a large chilled mixing bowl. Use a wooden spoon to stir ice cream to soften slightly. Stir in pumpkin, brown sugar, and pumpkin pie spice or cinnamon. Fold in whipped cream. Spoon ice cream mixture into cooled crust. Freeze about 3 hours, or till firm. Let stand 20 minutes and remove sides of springform pan before serving.

Makes 10 servings

Per serving: 343 calories, 2 g protein, 34 g carbohydrate, 23 g total fat (9 g saturated), 44 mg cholesterol, 148 mg sodium, 212 mg potassium

Dust each slice of this frosty pie with freshly grated nutmeg. A tangle of shredded orange peel adds color.

Frozen Margarita Pie

Preparation Time: 30 minutes
Baking Time: 5 minutes
Freezing Time: 4 hours

INGREDIENTS

PRETZEL CRUST

1	CUP FINELY CRUSHED PRETZELS
1/4	CUP SUGAR
1/3	CUP MARGARINE *OR* BUTTER, MELTED

FILLING

1	14-OUNCE CAN SWEETENED CONDENSED MILK
1/3	CUP FROZEN LIMEADE CONCENTRATE, THAWED
1	TO 2 TABLESPOONS TEQUILA
1	TABLESPOON ORANGE LIQUEUR
	SEVERAL DROPS GREEN FOOD COLORING (OPTIONAL)
1	CUP WHIPPING CREAM
	LIME SLICES (OPTIONAL)

40

Try this unique pie on a warm night after a spicy Mexican meal.

*T*he salty crust will remind you of the traditional salted rim of a margarita glass. A creamy lime-and-tequila filling completes this refreshing, tangy-sweet frozen pie.

■ For pretzel crust, stir together crushed pretzels and sugar. Stir in melted margarine or butter. Spread mixture evenly into a 9-inch pie plate. Press onto bottom and sides to form a firm, even crust. Bake in a preheated 375° oven for 5 minutes or till edge is lightly browned. Cool on a rack.

■ For filling, in a large mixing bowl combine sweetened condensed milk, limeade concentrate, tequila, orange liqueur, and, if desired, food coloring. In a medium mixing bowl beat whipping cream till soft peaks form; fold into tequila mixture. Spoon filling into crust. Cover and freeze about 4 hours, or till firm. Let stand 10 minutes before serving. If desired, garnish with lime slices.

Makes 8 servings

Per serving: 475 calories, 7 g protein, 57 g carbohydrate, 25 g total fat (12 g saturated), 64 mg cholesterol, 356 mg sodium, 291 mg potassium

Asparagus-Chicken Quiche

Place sliced tomatoes and salad greens alongside each slice of this savory pie for a light entrée.

Preparation Time: 50 minutes
Baking Time: 67 to 73 minutes

INGREDIENTS

6	ASPARAGUS SPEARS
	PASTRY FOR SINGLE-CRUST PIE (PAGE 14)
2	TABLESPOONS SNIPPED FRESH CHIVES OR GREEN ONION TOPS
3	BEATEN EGGS
1-1/2	CUPS MILK
1/8	TEASPOON SALT
1/8	TEASPOON PEPPER
1/2	CUP CHOPPED COOKED CHICKEN OR TURKEY
4	SLICES BACON, CRISP-COOKED, DRAINED, AND CRUMBLED
1-1/2	CUPS SHREDDED CHEDDAR CHEESE (6 OUNCES)
1	TABLESPOON ALL-PURPOSE FLOUR

41

*Q*uiche *is always a good choice for the centerpiece of a brunch or luncheon. To save time, make the pie crust dough the day before; cover and refrigerate it until needed.*

■ Wash asparagus; break off woody bases (spears should be about 4½ inches long). Cook asparagus spears in boiling water for 5 minutes; drain and set aside.

■ Prepare pastry as directed, except stir in chives or green onions with the flour and salt. Roll out dough to a 13-inch circle. Ease pastry into a 10x1-inch quiche dish; trim edge. Line *unpricked* pastry shell with a double thickness of heavy-duty aluminum foil. Bake in a preheated 450° oven for 8 minutes. Remove foil and bake for 4 to 5 minutes more, or till pastry is set and dry. Remove from oven. Reduce oven temperature to 325°.

■ Meanwhile, in a large mixing bowl stir together eggs, milk, salt, and pepper. Stir in chicken or turkey and bacon. In a medium mixing bowl toss together cheese and flour. Sprinkle cheese mixture over bottom of hot pastry shell. Carefully pour egg mixture into pastry shell. Arrange asparagus in spoke or fan pattern on top of the egg mixture. Bake in the 325° oven for 55 to 60 minutes, or till a knife inserted near the center comes out clean. Let stand 10 to 15 minutes before cutting into wedges.

Makes 6 servings

Per serving: 427 calories, 20 g protein, 24 g carbohydrate, 28 g total fat (11 g saturated), 156 mg cholesterol, 451 mg sodium, 280 mg potassium

Mexican Taco Pie

INGREDIENTS

PIE

	PASTRY FOR SINGLE-CRUST PIE (PAGE 14)
1/2	CUP FINELY CRUSHED CORN CHIPS
1/4	TEASPOON CRUSHED RED PEPPER (OPTIONAL)
1	POUND GROUND BEEF
1/2	CUP CHOPPED ONION
2	CLOVES GARLIC, MINCED
2	TEASPOONS CHILI POWDER
1/4	TEASPOON SALT
1/4	TEASPOON GROUND CUMIN
1	16-OUNCE CAN TOMATOES, CUT UP (UNDRAINED)
1	4-OUNCE CAN DICED GREEN CHILI PEPPERS, DRAINED
1/2	OF AN 8-OUNCE PACKAGE CREAM CHEESE, CUBED
1	8-OUNCE CAN RED KIDNEY BEANS, RINSED AND DRAINED
1	BEATEN EGG

GARNISH

1	CUP SHREDDED LETTUCE
1/2	CUP SHREDDED CHEDDAR CHEESE
1	MEDIUM TOMATO, CHOPPED (1 CUP)
1/3	CUP DAIRY SOUR CREAM
1/4	CUP COARSELY CRUSHED CORN CHIPS

*C*rushed corn chips in the crust give this dinner pie extra flavor and crunch. For variety, experiment with white, yellow, and even blue corn chips in the pastry and on top.

■ For pie, prepare pastry as directed, *except* stir in ½ cup crushed corn chips and, if desired, the crushed red pepper with the flour and salt. Roll out and line a 9-inch pie plate with pastry. Trim and crimp edge of pastry.

■ In a 10-inch skillet cook beef, onion, and garlic till meat is brown and onion is tender. Drain off fat. Stir in chili powder, salt, and cumin. Stir in *undrained* tomatoes, chili peppers, cream cheese, and kidney beans. Stir till cheese is melted. Stir about *1 cup* of the meat mixture into egg. Return all to skillet and mix well. Transfer filling to pie shell. To prevent overbrowning, cover edge of pie with foil. Bake in a preheated 375° oven for 25 minutes. Remove foil and bake about 20 minutes more, or till heated through and crust is golden. Let stand 10 minutes before serving.

■ For garnish, top pie with lettuce, cheese, tomato, sour cream, and ¼ cup corn chips.

Makes 6 to 8 servings

Per serving: 577 calories, 25 g protein, 37 g carbohydrate, 38 g total fat (15 g saturated), 119 mg cholesterol, 681 mg sodium, 615 mg potassium

Preparation Time: 35 minutes
Cooking Time: 5 minutes
Baking Time: 45 minutes

STEPS AT A GLANCE	Page
MAKING PIE PASTRY	8–14
BASIC CRIMPING	16

42

Spicy Mexican ingredients taste even better when baked in a savory pie shell. Crimp the edge simply for this casual main dish.

Two-Crust Pies

Steps for Finishing Two-Crust Pies

BASIC TOOLS FOR VENTING AND TRANSFERRING

A pie plate and rolling pin for the bottom pastry, plus sharp kitchen scissors and a knife for the top crust, are the everyday tools needed for finishing two-crust pies.

ROLLING PIN

PARING KNIFE

KITCHEN SCISSORS

9-INCH
PIE PLATE

44

VENTING AND TRANSFERRING
THE TOP CRUST

A TWO-CRUST PIE differs from a one-crust pie in more ways than just having extra pastry. First, the bottom crust is usually trimmed flush with the pie pan, rather than being folded under, to decrease its bulk. Secondly, the filling is almost always spooned in *before* trimming the dough. If done after trimming, its weight could drag the edge of the crust below the pan rim. Finally, the top crust is vented to let steam escape during baking. Any small opening works, but the simple and elegant sand-dollar pattern, shown on the facing page, is very effective. Cut the slits with a sharp, thin-bladed knife, such as a paring knife, after the top crust has been rolled out, but before it is transferred to the pie. Another way to fashion vents is with a lattice top or with a pattern of dots similar to that used on page 47, step 3, or with a small cutout, such as the one on page 60. Once the top crust is vented, gently place it on the pie, fold the edge under, and crimp as desired.

reroll the scraps of dough to decorate the top crust, if desired

STEP 1 TRIMMING THE BOTTOM CRUST

Set the bottom crust in the pie plate and ease it in without stretching the dough. Add the filling. With sharp kitchen scissors or a knife, trim away the excess dough flush with the outside edge of the plate.

do not cut slits if you are using
the other top crust variations
shown on the following pages

you can also transfer the crust, as
shown on page 11, step 4, by folding
the dough in quarters, then placing it
over the pie and unfolding it

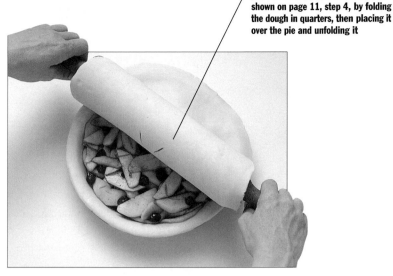

STEP 2 CUTTING SLITS IN THE TOP CRUST

After rolling the top crust about 1 inch in diameter larger than the pie plate, form steam vents by cutting several slits with a sharp knife. Widen the holes with the knife, or they will close when baked.

STEP 3 TRANSFERRING THE TOP CRUST

Drape the dough over the rolling pin. Lay the pin over the far edge of the filled pie and unroll the dough toward you, making sure that the crust is centered and there is an equal amount of dough hanging over the sides of the pan.

45

at this point,
the edge can be
crimped as for
a one-crust pie,
page 16

STEP 4 FOLDING THE EDGES UNDER

Trim the top crust to ½ inch from the edge of the pie plate. Working in a circle, lift the bottom crust and tuck the top crust under it. This will create a thick border for crimping.

This Apple-Cranberry Pie features a rope edge (page 17) and a traditional sand-dollar vent pattern. The recipe can be found on page 61.

Steps for Finishing Two-Crust Pies

SMALL
BOWL

PASTRY BRUSH

PIZZA CUTTER

RULER

SMALL
HORS D'OEUVRE
CUTTERS

FLUTED
PASTRY WHEEL

TOOTHPICKS OR SKEWERS

46

BASIC TOOLS FOR TWO-CRUST PIE TOPS

Use small tools such as hors d'oeuvre cutters, wooden skewers, a pastry wheel, or a pizza cutter to create pie lattice and decorations. A small bowl and brush are needed for applying glazes, and a ruler for making straight strips.

LATTICE VARIATIONS, DOTTED TOP, APPLIQUÉS, AND EGG GLAZING

YOU CAN EMBELLISH the detail on a two-crust pie top easily with a few elementary techniques. The ideas shown on these two pages look spectacular and require minimal effort. The first two trick the eye by looking like a true lattice, but in fact they are not. Another transforms the crust with a delicate pattern of dots punched out of the dough with a wooden pick. The fourth produces a very professional-looking pie, but is actually created with pastry cutouts shaped with a cookie cutter or traced freehand.

Remember that any decorative perforations, whether windows of lattice or lacy dots, eliminate the need for cutting vents. Always use double-crust pastry, and start with the bottom crust filled and trimmed as shown on page 44. For a simple glaze that will develop an attractive sheen all over the top crust, brush on a beaten egg white. For more color, use a whole egg or egg yolk mixed with water or cream. The richer the glaze, the browner the crust will be after baking.

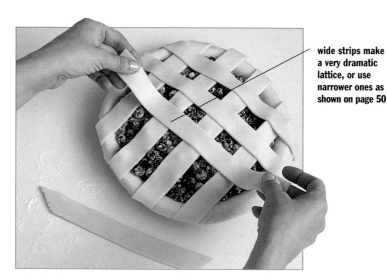

wide strips make a very dramatic lattice, or use narrower ones as shown on page 50

STEP 1 MAKING EASY LATTICE

To form a nonwoven lattice, cut plain (or pinked-edge) strips of dough from the pastry for the top crust. Lay half of the strips over the filling, then cross with the remaining strips. Trim them to the edge of bottom crust and brush ends with water. Fold bottom crust over, press slightly to seal, and crimp as desired.

be sure to align the cutout boxes or you will lose the effect

STEP 2 CREATING A CUTOUT LATTICE

Roll out the top crust on a floured surface into a circle about 1 inch larger in diameter than the pie plate. Cut out squares with a floured straight-edged or fluted cutter, starting in the center and working out to the edge.

make a simple herringbone edge by trimming bottom and top crust flush with the edge of the pan, then impressing at alternating angles with a fork

STEP 3 MAKING A DOTTED TOP

Set the top crust in place. With a floured toothpick or wooden skewer, punch out the design. Space the holes evenly for maximum effect. If you don't flour the toothpick, it will create a ragged opening.

STEP 4 DECORATING WITH APPLIQUÉS

Cut designs of desired shape from pastry scraps; use cutters or work freehand. Brush the top with water just until moist. Gently set the cutouts on the crust.

47

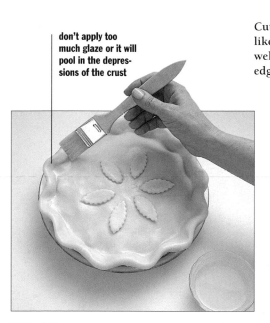

don't apply too much glaze or it will pool in the depressions of the crust

STEP 5 BRUSHING ON GLAZE

Dip a soft brush into the glaze and carefully apply to the entire top surface, including the edge. Make sure that no spots are missed, or that area will appear dull when baked. Wait until *after* glazing to cut vents or they may close up. To make the vents, cut small slits in the top crust right next to the appliqué so that the vents don't show.

Cutout pastry leaves, arranged like spokes of a wheel, pair well with the softly scalloped edge of this two-crust pie.

Steps for Finishing Two-Crust Pies

MAKING A WOVEN LATTICE

A TRADITIONAL LATTICE is perhaps the most stunning example of a decorative top, but this woven crust only looks difficult. Actually, it is simple to execute once the pattern is understood, and it makes a magnificent cover for all kinds of fillings, particularly fruit mixtures. Just weave the strips of dough over the filling, working from the center to the edges, then secure them with the overhanging bottom crust. The pattern is developed by working methodically, always folding back the strips that are *under* the perpendicular strip, laying a strip across, then straightening the folded strips.

Unlike other two-crust pies, the bottom crust of a lattice-topped pie is not trimmed flush to the pie pan, but rather left with a ½-inch margin like a one-crust pie. Crimp the edge in any fashion; ropes and rickracks look particularly good.

Fruit fillings tend to bubble up through the openings in lattice and flow over the sides of the pie onto the oven floor. To catch the juices and save cleanup, bake these pies on a round pizza pan if you have one. A round pan permits a more even flow of air around the pie than a rectangular cookie sheet, so the pie bakes more uniformly.

A lattice pattern can be changed dramatically by changing the width of its strips, by cutting strips with straight, rather than fluted edges (see Cherry-Berry Lattice Pie, page 58), by the amount of separation between the strips, or by placing the strips on the diagonal to form diamond-shaped, rather than square, spaces. The easiest lattice isn't woven at all. See page 46, step 1, for directions.

48

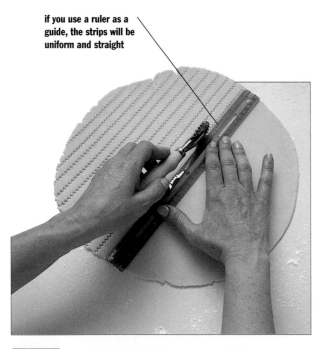

if you use a ruler as a guide, the strips will be uniform and straight

STEP 1 CUTTING THE STRIPS

Roll out dough for the top crust on a lightly floured surface. Cut ½-inch-wide strips with a fluted pastry wheel, a plain pastry wheel or pizza cutter, or a knife.

don't stretch the strips as you pick them up or they will shrink when baked

use the longer strips in the center of the pie, the shorter ones toward the edge

STEP 2 STARTING THE LATTICE

Trim bottom crust to ½ inch beyond edge of pie plate and fill. Lay one long strip of lattice across the center of the filling. Set a second strip perpendicular to the first strip. Then, add two more strips, one on either side of the first.

fold back the strips that are *under* the perpendicular strip, then place the next row of lattice

unfold the bent strips, then fold back the alternate ones to lay down the next piece

STEP 3 **WEAVING THE LATTICE STRIPS**

Fold back the middle strip. Lay another strip underneath it and over the two remaining strips. Straighten the folded strips; repeat on the other side. Then fold back the two strips that are *under* the perpendicular strip; lay another strip across, and straighten the strips. Repeat in each direction, from the center.

49

A traditional lattice crust takes time, but the results are spectacular. The recipe for the Cherry-Berry Lattice Pie shown here is on page 58.

don't trim the strips until the entire lattice has been woven

STEP 4 **FINISHING THE LATTICE**

Continue working from the center of the pie out to the edges until all the strips have been used or until the filling is completely covered with the lattice. As you get toward the edge, the strips will have more overhang.

STEP 5 **FOLDING THE EDGE OF THE CRUST**

Trim the strips flush with the inside edge of the bottom crust. Brush the ends of the strips with water. Fold the excess dough over the strips, pinching to seal. Crimp as desired.

50

A cross between a brownie and a
hot-fudge sundae, this rich dessert
is best topped with a scoop of ice
cream and fresh or candied cherries.

Brownie Crostata with Hot Fudge Sauce

INGREDIENTS

BROWNIE CROSTATA

1/2	CUP MARGARINE OR BUTTER
3	OUNCES UNSWEETENED CHOCOLATE, CUT UP
3	BEATEN EGGS
1-1/2	CUPS SUGAR
1/2	CUP ALL-PURPOSE FLOUR
1	TEASPOON VANILLA
1	CUP CHOPPED PECANS
	PASTRY FOR DOUBLE-CRUST PIE (PAGE 14)

HOT FUDGE SAUCE

3/4	CUP SEMISWEET CHOCOLATE PIECES OR CHOPPED SEMISWEET CHOCOLATE
1/4	CUP MARGARINE OR BUTTER
2/3	CUP SUGAR
1	5-OUNCE CAN EVAPORATED MILK (2/3 CUP)

*B*ake this scrumptious brownie in pastry for the choco-late-lover in your life. Use an easy lattice top (page 46); the filling is too sticky for a woven lattice.

■ For brownie crostata, in a small, heavy saucepan melt margarine or butter and chocolate over low heat, stirring frequently. Cool for 20 minutes. In a large mixing bowl combine eggs, sugar, flour, and vanilla. Beat smooth with rotary beater or whisk. Stir in cooled chocolate and pecans.

■ Prepare and roll out pastry as directed. Line a 9-inch pie plate with half of the pastry. Transfer filling to pastry-lined pie plate; trim pastry to ½ inch beyond edge of pie plate. Cut top pastry as directed for easy lattice. Trim, seal, and crimp edge of pastry. Bake in a preheated 350° oven for 50 to 55 minutes, or till a knife inserted near center comes out clean. Cool slightly on a rack.

■ For hot fudge sauce, in a small, heavy saucepan melt chocolate and margarine or butter, stirring often. Add sugar; gradually stir in evaporated milk. Bring to boiling; reduce heat. Boil gently over low heat for 8 minutes, stirring often. Remove from heat. Serve warm over crostata.

Makes 8 to 10 servings

Per serving: 905 calories, 11 g protein, 98 g carbohydrate, 57 g total fat (12 g saturated), 86 mg cholesterol, 382 mg sodium, 328 mg potassium

Preparation Time: 55 minutes
Baking Time: 50 to 55 minutes
Cooking Time: 10 minutes

STEPS AT A GLANCE	Page
MAKING PIE PASTRY	8–14
MAKING EASY LATTICE	46
BASIC CRIMPING	16
MAKING HOT FUDGE SAUCE	51

51

STEPS FOR MAKING HOT FUDGE SAUCE

STEP 1 MELTING CHOCOLATE
Place chocolate pieces in a small saucepan along with the margarine or butter. Cook over low heat, stirring with a wooden spoon to blend the ingredients as they melt. Keep the temperature low at this point, or the chocolate may separate.

STEP 2 BOILING THE MIXTURE
Mix in sugar and gradually stir in evaporated milk. Increase the heat just until the sauce boils, then reduce heat quickly and cook gently until done, stirring frequently.

52

Widely spaced scallops and six
teardrop-shaped vents give this
top crust a graceful appearance.

Sugar-crusted Strawberry-Rhubarb Pie

INGREDIENTS

1-1/4	CUPS SUGAR
3	TABLESPOONS QUICK-COOKING TAPIOCA
3	CUPS STRAWBERRIES, SLICED
2	CUPS FRESH OR FROZEN UNSWEET-ENED SLICED RHUBARB
1/2	TEASPOON FINELY SHREDDED ORANGE PEEL
1/2	TEASPOON GROUND CINNAMON
1/4	TEASPOON GROUND NUTMEG
12	SMALL SUGAR CUBES, OR 1/4 CUP SANDING OR PEARL SUGAR
	PASTRY FOR DOUBLE-CRUST PIE (PAGE 14)

*M*any cooks prefer tapioca to flour or cornstarch for baking pies because tapioca creates a clear, juicy pie filling that won't become watery if frozen.

■ In a large mixing bowl combine sugar and tapioca. Add strawberries, rhubarb, orange peel, cinnamon, and nutmeg. Toss gently till fruit is coated. Let mixture stand about 15 minutes, or till a syrup forms, stirring occasionally.

■ Meanwhile, coarsely crush sugar cubes if using; set aside. Prepare and roll out pastry as directed. Line a 9-inch pie plate with half of pastry. Stir fruit mixture; transfer to pastry-lined pie plate; trim pastry even with rim. Cut slits in top crust. Place crust on filling. Trim, seal, and crimp edge of pastry. Brush top crust with water; sprinkle with crushed sugar cubes or sanding or pearl sugar.

■ To prevent overbrowning, cover edge of pie with foil. Bake in a preheated 375° oven for 25 minutes. Remove foil and bake for 20 to 25 minutes more, or till top is golden. Cool on a rack.

Makes 8 servings

Per serving: 427 calories, 4 g protein, 67 g carbohydrate, 18 g total fat (4 g saturated), 0 mg cholesterol, 136 mg sodium, 213 mg potassium

Preparation Time: 35 minutes
Baking Time: 45 to 50 minutes

STEPS FOR CRUSHING SUGAR

STEP 1 CRUSHING SUGAR

Place sugar cubes inside a heavy-duty plastic bag. Pound the cubes with a rolling pin until coarsely crushed.

STEP 2 SPRINKLING SUGAR

Brush the top crust with water, then sprinkle with crushed sugar. Or, use opaque pearl sugar (left dish) or translucent sanding sugar (right dish), available from baking supply catalogs or cake decorating stores.

Caramel-Apple Pie

Preparation Time: 1 hour
Cooking Time: 5 minutes
Baking Time: 45 to 50 minutes

INGREDIENTS

CARAMEL SAUCE

1/2	CUP PACKED BROWN SUGAR
1	TABLESPOON CORNSTARCH
1/4	CUP WATER
1/3	CUP HALF-AND-HALF OR LIGHT CREAM
2	TABLESPOONS LIGHT CORN SYRUP
1	TABLESPOON MARGARINE OR BUTTER
1/2	TEASPOON VANILLA

PIE

1/2	CUP SUGAR
3	TABLESPOONS ALL-PURPOSE FLOUR
1/4	TEASPOON GROUND CINNAMON
1/8	TEASPOON GROUND NUTMEG
6	CUPS THINLY SLICED, PEELED COOKING APPLES (6 MEDIUM)
1/2	CUP RAISINS
1/2	CUP CARAMEL SAUCE (ABOVE)
	PASTRY FOR DOUBLE-CRUST PIE (PAGE 14)

PASTRY CUTOUTS

1	EGG YOLK
1/4	TEASPOON WATER
3 OR 4	DROPS RED FOOD COLORING
3 OR 4	DROPS GREEN FOOD COLORING

*U*se pastry cutouts appropriate to the season or holiday if you wish; for example, try autumn leaves for Thanksgiving or shooting stars for Independence Day. To cut down on preparation time, use bottled caramel sauce instead of homemade.

■ For caramel sauce, in a heavy small saucepan mix brown sugar and cornstarch. Stir in water. Stir in half-and-half or light cream and light corn syrup. Cook and stir till bubbly (mixture may appear curdled). Cook and stir for 2 minutes more. Remove from heat; stir in margarine or butter and vanilla. Cover surface and cool without stirring.

■ For pie, in a large mixing bowl combine sugar, flour, cinnamon, and nutmeg. Add apples and raisins. Pour ½ cup of the caramel sauce over apple mixture; reserve remaining sauce to serve with pie. Toss gently till apples are coated. Prepare and roll out pastry as directed. Line a 9-inch pie plate with half of the pastry. Transfer filling to pastry-lined pie plate; trim pastry even with rim. Cut slits or vents in top crust. Place crust on filling. Trim, seal, and crimp edge of pastry.

■ For pastry cutouts, use a small hors d'oeuvre cutter or sharp knife to cut out apples and leaves from pastry scraps. Brush top crust with water. Arrange pastry cutouts on top crust. Mix egg yolk with ¼ teaspoon water. Divide yolk mixture in half. Add red food coloring to one half and green food coloring to the other half; mix well. With a clean, small paintbrush, paint pastry cutouts with 2 coats of color. To prevent overbrowning, cover the edge of the pie with foil. Bake in a preheated 375° oven for 25 minutes. Remove foil and bake for 20 to 25 minutes more, or till top is golden and apples are tender. Cool on a rack.

Makes 8 servings

Per serving: 465 calories, 4 g protein, 71 g carbohydrate, 20 g total fat (5 g saturated), 2 mg cholesterol, 161 mg sodium, 232 mg potassium

STEP FOR MAKING COLORED APPLIQUÉS

STEP 1 PAINTING CUTOUTS
Cut out pastry apples and leaves, or other shapes, with small cutters or freehand with a knife. Brush the top crust with water and apply the cutouts. Mix egg yolk and water, then place in two small cups; add red food coloring to one batch and green food coloring to the other. With a clean paint brush, color the cutouts, then apply a second coat. If you can find it, paste food coloring will yield a more intense hue than liquid coloring. Look for it at better cookware stores and cake decorating supply stores.

54

To complement the apple cutouts,
try a large round central vent and neat
rickracks to decorate this pie.

Spiced Blueberry Pie

INGREDIENTS

1/2	CUP GRANULATED SUGAR
1/3	CUP PACKED BROWN SUGAR
1/3	CUP CORNSTARCH
1	TEASPOON FINELY SHREDDED LEMON PEEL
1/2	TEASPOON GROUND CINNAMON
1/4	TEASPOON GROUND ALLSPICE
	DASH GROUND CLOVES
6	CUPS FRESH *OR* FROZEN BLUEBERRIES
	PASTRY FOR DOUBLE-CRUST PIE (PAGE 14)
	MILK
	GRANULATED SUGAR

Preparation Time: 25 minutes
Baking Time: 45 to 80 minutes

STEPS AT A GLANCE	Page
MAKING PIE PASTRY	8–14
VENTING & TRANSFERRING THE TOP CRUST	44
APPLYING CUTOUTS	18
MAKING A DOTTED TOP	47

*T*he spices in this pie make it special, but if you're hooked on tradition, omit the cinnamon, allspice, and cloves. The milk and sugar on top glaze the crust beautifully.

■ In a large mixing bowl combine ½ cup granulated sugar, the brown sugar, cornstarch, lemon peel, cinnamon, allspice, and cloves. Add fresh or frozen blueberries. Toss gently till berries are coated. (If using frozen berries, let stand 15 to 30 minutes, or till berries are partially thawed but still icy.)

■ Prepare and roll out pastry as directed. Line a 9-inch pie plate with half of the pastry. Stir berry mixture; transfer to pastry-lined pie plate. Cut slits in top crust. Place crust on filling. Trim, seal, and crimp edge of pastry. Brush crust with milk and sprinkle with granulated sugar.

■ To prevent overbrowning, cover the edge of the pie with foil. Bake in a preheated 375° oven for 25 minutes (50 minutes for frozen berries). Remove foil and bake for 20 to 25 minutes more for fresh berries (20 to 30 minutes for frozen berries), or till top is golden. Cool on a rack.

Makes 8 servings

Per serving: 421 calories, 4 g protein, 64 g carbohydrate, 18 g total fat (4 g saturated), 0 mg cholesterol, 145 mg sodium, 163 mg potassium

56

Give this pastry a homespun look with a dotted top of hearts and ovals. A necklace of tiny cutout circles, made with a round pastry tip, frames the design.

Ginger-Peach Pie

Spicy and wholesome, this pie tastes great with a bit of extra chopped crystallized ginger scattered on top.

Preparation Time: 30 minutes
Baking Time: 45 to 80 minutes

INGREDIENTS

1/2	TO 3/4 CUP SUGAR
3	TABLESPOONS ALL-PURPOSE FLOUR
2	TABLESPOONS FINELY CHOPPED CRYSTALLIZED GINGER
1/4	TEASPOON GROUND MACE
6	CUPS THINLY SLICED PEELED PEACHES *OR* FROZEN UNSWEET-ENED PEACH SLICES
	PASTRY FOR DOUBLE-CRUST PIE (PAGE 14)
	MILK
	SUGAR

*C*rystallized ginger adds a spicy-sweet flavor and a gentle touch of heat to this chunky pie filling. Whole wheat flour added to the crust gives it a hearty texture.

■ In a large mixing bowl combine the ½ to ¾ cup sugar, the flour, crystallized ginger, and mace. Add fresh or frozen peaches. Toss gently till peaches are coated. (If using frozen peaches, let stand for 15 to 30 minutes, or till peaches are partially thawed but still icy.)

■ Prepare pastry as directed, *except* substitute ¾ cup *whole-wheat flour* for ¾ cup of the all-purpose flour. Line a 9-inch pie plate with half of the pastry. Stir peach mixture; transfer to pastry-lined pie plate. Trim pastry even with rim. Cut slits in top crust. Place crust on filling. Trim, seal, and crimp edge of pastry. Brush with milk and sprinkle with sugar. To prevent overbrowning, cover edge of pie with foil. Bake in a preheated 375° oven for 25 minutes for fresh peaches (50 minutes for frozen peaches). Remove foil and bake for 20 to 25 minutes more for fresh peaches (20 to 30 minutes for frozen peaches), or till top is golden. Cool on a rack.

Makes 8 servings

Per serving: 377 calories, 4 g protein, 53 g carbohydrate, 18 g total fat (4 g saturated), 0 mg cholesterol, 136 mg sodium, 289 mg potassium

Cherry-Berry Lattice Pie

Weave narrow strips of pastry into a traditional lattice for this summertime treat. Score the edge of the crust with the point of a knife at even intervals.

Preparation Time: 40 minutes
Baking Time: 45 to 80 minutes

INGREDIENTS

1	TO 1-1/4 CUPS SUGAR
1/3	CUP ALL-PURPOSE FLOUR
3	CUPS FRESH *OR* FROZEN RED RASPBERRIES
2	CUPS FRESH *OR* FROZEN UNSWEETENED PITTED TART RED CHERRIES
1/4	TEASPOON ALMOND EXTRACT
	PASTRY FOR DOUBLE-CRUST PIE (PAGE 14)

*T*art with cherries and sweet with raspberries, this pie is a crowd-pleaser. Choose the low end of the sugar range if you like a tart pie, the higher amount if you prefer a sweet one.

STEPS AT A GLANCE	Page
MAKING PIE PASTRY	8–14
MAKING A WOVEN LATTICE	48
BASIC CRIMPING	16

■ In a large mixing bowl combine sugar and flour. Add raspberries, cherries, and almond extract. Toss gently till fruit is coated. (If using frozen fruit, let stand for 15 to 30 minutes, or till fruit is partially thawed but still icy.)

■ Prepare and roll out pastry as directed. Line a 9-inch pie plate with half of the pastry. Stir filling; transfer to pastry-lined pie plate. Trim pastry to ½ inch beyond edge of pie plate. Cut top crust as directed for a woven lattice. Trim, seal, and crimp edge of pastry. To prevent overbrowning, cover edge of pie with foil. Bake in a preheated 375° oven 25 minutes for fresh fruit (50 minutes for frozen fruit). Remove foil and bake 20 to 25 minutes more for fresh fruit (20 to 30 minutes for frozen), or till top is golden. Cool on a rack.

Makes 8 servings

Per serving: 405 calories, 4 g protein, 60 g carbohydrate, 18 g total fat (4 g saturated), 0 mg cholesterol, 136 mg sodium, 173 mg potassium

Glazed Pineapple-Rhubarb Pie

*R*hubarb *is such a natural ingredient for pie that it's sometimes referred to as pieplant. Here it's teamed with pineapple, a fruit that's seldom found in pies.*

■ Drain pineapple, reserving *1 tablespoon* of the juice. In a large mixing bowl combine pineapple, rhubarb, sugar, flour, and lemon juice. (If using frozen rhubarb, let mixture stand for 15 to 20 minutes, or till the rhubarb is partially thawed but still icy.)

■ Prepare and roll out pastry as directed. Line a 9-inch pie plate with half of the pastry. Transfer filling to pastry-lined pie plate; trim pastry even with rim. Cut slits in top crust. Place crust on filling. Trim, seal, and crimp edge of pastry.

■ To prevent overbrowning, cover edge of pie with foil. Bake in a preheated 375° oven for 25 minutes (50 minutes for frozen rhubarb). Remove foil and bake for 25 to 30 minutes more, or till top is golden.

■ In a small mixing bowl combine powdered sugar and enough of the reserved pineapple juice (1 to 2 teaspoons) to make a glaze of drizzling consistency. Drizzle glaze over hot pie. Cool on a rack.

Makes 8 servings

Per serving: 427 calories, 4 g protein, 65 g carbohydrate, 18 g total fat (4 g saturated), 0 mg cholesterol, 137 mg sodium, 212 mg potassium

Preparation Time: 40 minutes
Baking Time: 50 to 80 minutes

STEPS AT A GLANCE	Page
MAKING PIE PASTRY	8–14
VENTING & TRANSFERRING THE TOP CRUST	44
BASIC CRIMPING	16

INGREDIENTS

1	20-OUNCE CAN CRUSHED PINEAPPLE (JUICE PACK)
2	CUPS SLICED FRESH *OR* FROZEN RHUBARB
1	CUP SUGAR
1/4	CUP ALL-PURPOSE FLOUR
1	TABLESPOON LEMON JUICE
	PASTRY FOR DOUBLE-CRUST PIE (PAGE 14)
1/4	CUP SIFTED POWDERED SUGAR

59

To give this pie a radiant appearance, press the edge with a spoon handle, then squeeze the tips into rickrack points. For vents, pierce the top in expanding circles with the corner of an oval hors d'oeuvre cutter.

Shaker-Style Lemon Pie

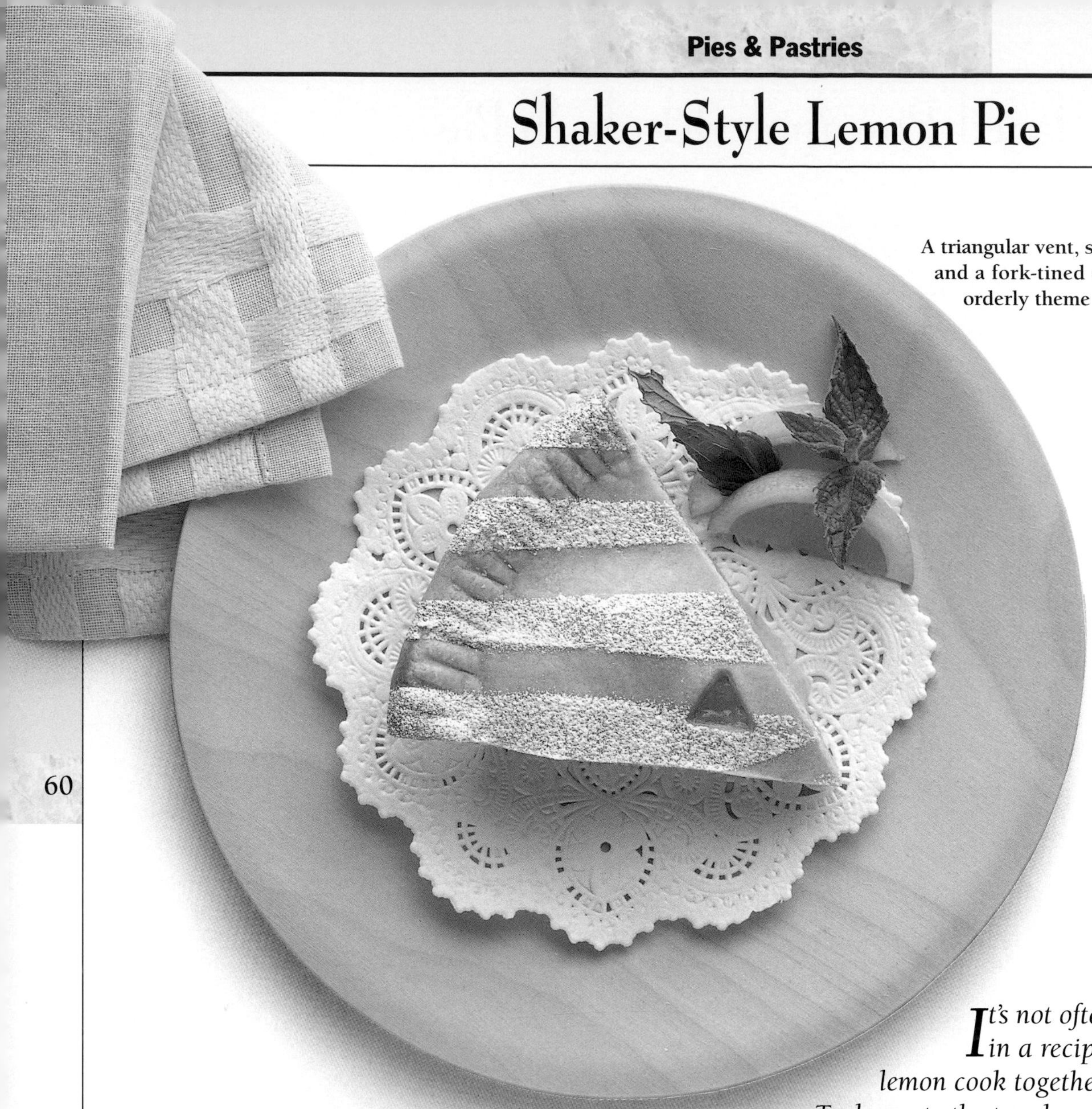

A triangular vent, stripes of powdered sugar,
and a fork-tined edge carry out the
orderly theme of a Shaker-style pie.

Preparation Time: 30 minutes
Baking Time: 35 to 40 minutes

INGREDIENTS

2	CUPS SUGAR
1/3	CUP ALL-PURPOSE FLOUR
1/8	TEASPOON SALT
2/3	CUP WATER
2	TABLESPOONS MARGARINE *OR* BUTTER, MELTED
3	SLIGHTLY BEATEN EGGS
2	TEASPOONS FINELY SHREDDED LEMON PEEL
2	LEMONS, PEELED, VERY THINLY SLICED, AND SEEDED
	PASTRY FOR DOUBLE-CRUST PIE (PAGE 14)
	SIFTED POWDERED SUGAR

*I*t's not often that the lemon's fruit is used
in a recipe. In this pie, thin slices of
lemon cook together into a thick, creamy filling.
To decorate the top, lay parallel strips of waxed paper a
few inches apart, dust with powdered sugar, then remove the strips.

60

■ In a large mixing bowl combine sugar, flour, and salt. Add water, margarine or butter, eggs, and lemon peel; stir till well combined. Gently stir in lemon slices.

■ Prepare and roll out pastry as directed. Line a 9-inch pie plate with half of the pastry. Transfer filling to pastry-lined pie plate; trim pastry even with rim. Cut slits in top crust. Place crust on filling. Trim, seal, and crimp edge of pastry.

■ To prevent overbrowning, cover edge of pie with foil. Bake in a preheated 400° oven for 25 minutes. Remove foil and bake for 10 to 15 minutes more, or till top is golden. Cool on a rack. Before serving, dust with powdered sugar. Store, covered, in the refrigerator.

Makes 8 servings

Per serving: 527 calories, 6 g protein, 79 g carbohydrate, 22 g total fat (5 g saturated), 80 mg cholesterol, 229 mg sodium, 102 mg potassium

Apple-Cranberry Pie

Preparation Time: 50 minutes
Cooking Time: 5 minutes
Baking Time: 50 to 55 minutes

INGREDIENTS

1	CUP CRANBERRIES
3/4	CUP SUGAR
2	TABLESPOONS APPLE CIDER, APPLE JUICE, *OR* ORANGE JUICE
1	TABLESPOON CORNSTARCH
1/2	CUP SUGAR
2	TABLESPOONS CORNSTARCH
1	TEASPOON APPLE PIE SPICE
1	TEASPOON FINELY SHREDDED ORANGE PEEL
5	CUPS THINLY SLICED, PEELED COOKING APPLES (5 MEDIUM APPLES)
	PASTRY FOR DOUBLE-CRUST PIE (PAGE 14)
	MILK
	SUGAR

*B*efore cranberry season is over, buy a couple of extra bags to stash in your freezer. Then you can bake this autumn pie any time of the year. Sprinkle the top crust with sanding sugar (see page 53), as shown here, or use granulated sugar.

■ In a small saucepan combine cranberries, ¾ cup sugar, apple cider, apple juice, or orange juice, and 1 tablespoon cornstarch. Bring to boiling. Boil gently for 5 minutes, stirring frequently. Cool 20 minutes.

■ In a large mixing bowl combine ½ cup sugar, 2 tablespoons cornstarch, the apple pie spice, and orange peel. Add the apples; toss to coat. Stir cooled cranberry mixture into apple mixture.

■ Prepare and roll out pastry as directed. Line a 9-inch pie plate with half of the pastry. Transfer filling to pastry-lined pie plate; trim pastry. Cut slits in top crust or create a cutout lattice. Place crust on filling. Trim, seal, and crimp edge of pastry. Brush top crust with milk; sprinkle with sugar.

■ To prevent overbrowning, cover edge of pie with foil. Bake in a preheated 375° oven for 25 minutes. Remove foil and bake for 25 to 30 minutes more, or till top is golden. Cool on a rack.

Makes 8 servings

Per serving: 435 calories, 3 g protein, 68 g carbohydrate, 18 g total fat (4 g saturated), 0 mg cholesterol, 136 mg sodium, 106 mg potassium

61

A cutout lattice allows a tantalizing peek at the glistening fruit that fills this pie. A wavy rope edge allows the juices to bubble up and settle in the crevices.

Tourtière

INGREDIENTS

FILLING

1	POUND GROUND PORK
1	LARGE CARROT, COARSELY SHREDDED (1 CUP)
1/2	CUP CHOPPED ONION
2	SLICES BACON, FINELY CHOPPED
2	MEDIUM POTATOES, PEELED AND CHOPPED (1-3/4 CUPS)
3/4	CUP BEEF BROTH
2	CLOVES GARLIC, MINCED
1	TEASPOON DRIED SAGE, CRUSHED
1/2	TEASPOON SALT
1/4	TEASPOON PEPPER

PASTRY

2	CUPS ALL-PURPOSE FLOUR
1/2	TEASPOON BAKING POWDER
1/2	TEASPOON DRIED THYME, CRUSHED
1/4	TEASPOON SALT
2/3	CUP SHORTENING *OR* BUTTER
1	BEATEN EGG
2	TABLESPOONS COLD WATER
1	TEASPOON LEMON JUICE

Preparation Time: 45 minutes
Cooking Time: 17 minutes
Baking Time: 25 to 30 minutes

62

*T*ourtière is a classic Canadian pork pie, often served on Christmas Eve. Its savory crust, seasoned with thyme, also would be good with your favorite chicken or beef pie filling.

■ For filling, in a large skillet cook pork, carrot, onion, and bacon till pork is brown and onion is tender. Drain off fat. In a medium saucepan combine potatoes, beef broth, and garlic. Bring to boiling. Reduce heat and simmer, covered, about 10 minutes, or till potatoes are tender. *Do not drain.* Mash potato mixture. Stir in pork mixture, sage, salt, and pepper. Set aside.

■ For pastry, stir together flour, baking powder, thyme, and salt. Cut in shortening or butter till pieces are the size of small peas. Set aside. Stir together egg, cold water, and lemon juice. Sprinkle egg mixture over flour mixture, 1 tablespoon at a time, tossing gently with a fork. Divide mixture in half. Shape each half into a ball. Roll out pastry. Line a 9-inch pie plate with half of the pastry. Transfer filling to pastry-lined pie plate. Cut slits in top crust. Place crust on filling. Trim, seal and crimp edge of pastry. Bake in a preheated 400° oven for 25 to 30 minutes, or till golden brown. Let stand for 10 minutes.

Makes 6 servings

Per serving: 516 calories, 17 g protein, 43 g carbohydrate, 31 g total fat (6 g saturated), 73 mg cholesterol, 472 mg sodium, 436 mg potassium

Serve wedges of this savory main dish with sautéed peppers and pea pods. Garnish with fresh thyme leaves, if desired.

STEPS AT A GLANCE	Page
MAKING PIE PASTRY	8–14
VENTING & TRANSFERRING THE TOP CRUST	44
BASIC CRIMPING	16

Tarts & Tartlets

Steps for Making Tarts

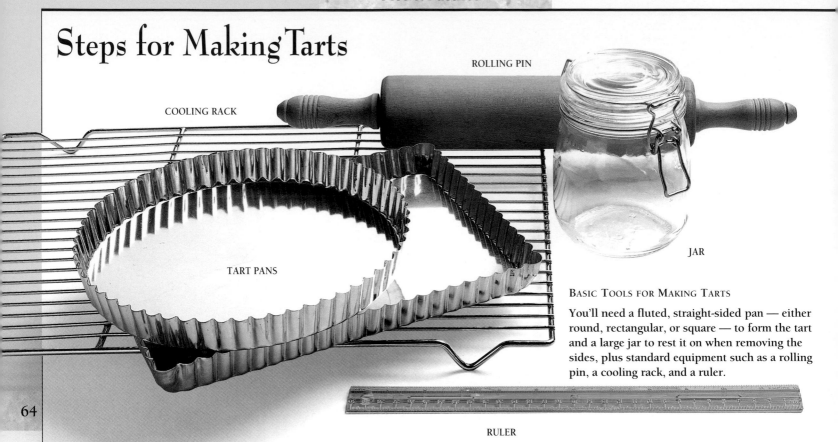

ROLLING PIN

COOLING RACK

JAR

TART PANS

BASIC TOOLS FOR MAKING TARTS

You'll need a fluted, straight-sided pan — either round, rectangular, or square — to form the tart and a large jar to rest it on when removing the sides, plus standard equipment such as a rolling pin, a cooling rack, and a ruler.

RULER

64

P IES AND TARTS are like fraternal, rather than identical, twins. There is a family resemblance, but they have important differences. Both pastries include flour, a liquid, and a fat. Unlike a pie crust, however, traditional tart pastry always is made with butter rather than shortening, and in a greater proportion, so much so that another name for tart pastry is "short" dough, meaning high in fat (like shortbread cookies). The extra fat coats the flour particles in the dough so that they absorb less liquid. As a result, the strands of structure-building proteins that develop when flour mixes with water are literally shorter than they would be otherwise. The crust bakes rich and crumbly, rather than flaky.

In addition to more fat, tart dough also incorporates egg yolks for strength and color, and often sugar for sweetness. On the other hand, this rich pastry may be overwhelming for some fillings, so a tart recipe may call for regular pie pastry, or even a cookie crust, for balance. Follow the recipe at right when a traditional tart crust is called for in this chapter.

TART PASTRY

INGREDIENTS

1-1/4	CUPS ALL-PURPOSE FLOUR
1/4	CUP SUGAR
1/2	CUP COLD BUTTER
2	BEATEN EGG YOLKS
1	TABLESPOON CHILLED WATER

■ In a medium mixing bowl stir together flour and sugar. Cut in butter till pieces are the size of small peas.

■ In a small mixing bowl stir together egg yolks and water. Gradually stir egg yolk mixture into flour mixture. Gently knead the dough just till a ball forms.

■ To prepare in a food processor, place the steel blade in the work bowl. Add flour, sugar, and butter. Process with on/off turns till pieces are the size of small peas. Stir together egg yolks and water. With machine running, quickly add liquid through the feed tube. Stop machine as soon as all liquid is added. Process with 2 more on/off turns. Remove dough and shape into a ball.

■ For easier handling, cover dough with plastic wrap and chill for 30 to 60 minutes. Use as directed in recipe.

use this measuring
technique for any
shape of tart

you can also fit the dough into
the pan with your fingers or the
heel of your hand rather than a
ball of dough

let some dough hang over
the side of the pan all the
way around

be sure that the dough is
fitted into the pan *before*
trimming, or the crust will
shrink when baked

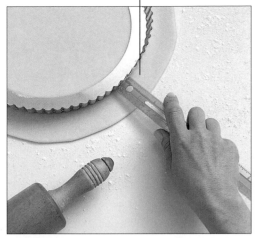

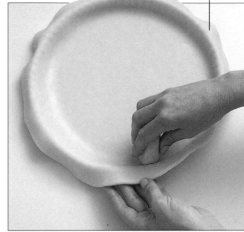

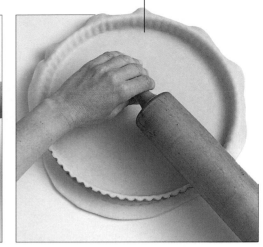

STEP 1 MEASURING THE DOUGH

Roll out dough on a floured surface to a circle
2 inches larger than the diameter of the tart
pan. To make sure that the dough circle is the
correct size, lay the pan on the dough and measure the margin with a ruler.

STEP 2 FITTING THE DOUGH IN THE PAN

Transfer the dough from the work surface to the
pan as for a one-crust pie, page 11. With one hand,
lift up a section of the overhanging dough and
ease into the pan. Use a small ball of dough, your
fingers, or the heel of your hand to push against
the inside of the dough so it fits snugly, especially
where bottom and sides meet.

STEP 3 TRIMMING WITH A ROLLING PIN

To remove excess dough, roll around the entire
edge of the pan with a rolling pin. Use an even,
smooth action. The overhanging dough will drop
off, leaving a neat edge.

65

push from the outside in so
that the inside edge of the pan
is fully covered with dough

a metal can or
any heatproof
sturdy container
will also work

STEP 4 TRIMMING WITH YOUR FINGERS

Instead of using a rolling pin, you can use your thumb
to trim away the extra dough. Lift up the dough with
one hand, and push across the rim of the tart pan with
the thumb of your other hand.

STEP 5 REMOVING THE SIDES OF THE PAN

When done, remove the baked tart from the oven; let cool
slightly. Set on a lidded jar. The sides of the tart pan will
fall away. Then carefully transfer the tart to a rack to cool
completely (leave the pan bottom in place).

Steps for Making Tartlets

MEDIUM
SAUCEPAN

BAKING SHEET

BASIC TOOLS FOR MAKING TARTLETS

For tartlets, have available 3-inch pans or
miniature muffin pans, a baking sheet, a rack,
and a saucepan and spoon for the filling.

MINI
MUFFIN PAN

COOLING RACK

SPOON

3-INCH TARTLET PANS

LIKE TARTS, TARTLETS look difficult because they are so
beautiful. In fact, they are easy to make because of
their small size, and it is their size that makes them so
appealing both to the cook and to whoever eats them.
There is less dough to handle, and most of the shaping
is done with your fingers. Dinner guests love dainty
tartlets because they make perfect finger food, and
because more than one is never enough!

Classic tartlet pans come in many shapes: squares,
circles, triangles, even tapered ovals that look like little
boats (called, appropriately, *barquettes*). Like full-sized
tart pans, some have convenient removable bottoms.
Tassies are homey tartlets shaped with the thumb in
miniature muffin cups. They resemble thimble-sized
tumblers, which could be a hint as to how they were
named: *tasse* means "cup" in French.

Before they are filled, tartlets are fully baked and
cooled. The crust is slightly crumbly, but will stand
without the support of a pan. However, they are still
very delicate; that is part of their appeal. Handle them
carefully or they may shatter.

If you have never made tartlets, a good introduction
would be the Lemon Curd–Raspberry Tartlets on page
76. Part of the tartlet assortment on the opposite page,
they have a tangy citrus filling and a raspberry garnish.
Or try the Orange-glazed Fruit Tartlets on page 77.

do not make the
bottom too thin
or the filling will
leak out

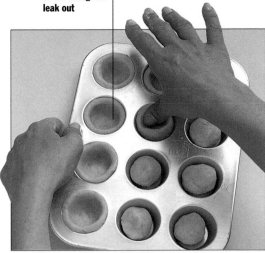

a baking sheet allows
small tart pans to be
transported easily

you can also roll
the dough into one
large round and
cut out smaller
rounds from it

STEP 1 FILLING MINI MUFFIN PANS

Form the dough into balls. Set a ball of dough into
each muffin cup. To shape, press evenly into the
dough with your thumb to create a shell.

STEP 2 FILLING TARTLET PANS

Divide the dough into balls, then roll each out into
a thin, round disc. Fit into the tartlet pan and trim
as for standard tarts, page 65, step 3 or 4.

if pans are in one piece,
remove the baked pastry
very carefully, then fill

if pans have remov-
able bottoms, leave
tartlets in the pans
while filling and
remove sides just
before serving

STEP 3 SPOONING IN THE FILLING

Let the baked tartlet shells cool in their pans on
a wire rack. Arrange the baked tartlet shells on a
serving plate and spoon in the filling.

Whether finished in a single bite or
several, tartlets have that special charm
found only in little things. You will find
Orange-glazed Fruit Tartlets on page 77 and
Lemon Curd–Raspberry Tartlets on page 76.

Very Berry–Cream Cheese Tart

Preparation Time: 50 minutes
Baking time: 5 minutes
Chilling Time: 4 to 6 hours

INGREDIENTS

CRUST

1	CUP FINELY CRUSHED GRAHAM CRACKERS (ABOUT 14 SQUARES)
3/4	CUP FINELY CRUSHED VANILLA WAFERS (18 TO 20 WAFERS)
1/4	CUP FINELY CHOPPED ALMONDS
1/3	CUP MARGARINE OR BUTTER, MELTED

FILLING

1	ENVELOPE UNFLAVORED GELATIN
2	CUPS UNSWEETENED CHERRY JUICE
2	5-OUNCE JARS CREAM CHEESE SPREAD WITH PINEAPPLE
1/4	CUP SIFTED POWDERED SUGAR
1	TEASPOON VANILLA
2	CUPS BLACKBERRIES
2	CUPS RASPBERRIES

*W*hen *making a pie filling that contains gelatin, you need to cool the mixture first until it is partially set before pouring it into the shell. To do this, you can either place the filling in the refrigerator for about an hour and stir occasionally, or cool the mixture in the pan directly over a bowl of ice water, which takes only about 15 minutes.*

■ For crust, in a medium mixing bowl combine crushed graham crackers, crushed vanilla wafers, and almonds. Add melted margarine or butter; toss to mix well. Spread mixture evenly into a 9-inch springform pan. Press onto bottom and 1½ inches up the sides to form a firm, even crust. Bake in a preheated 375° oven for 5 minutes. Cool on a rack.

■ For filling, in a medium saucepan combine gelatin and cherry juice; let stand for 5 minutes to soften. Cook and stir over low heat till gelatin dissolves. Set the saucepan in a large bowl of ice water for about 15 minutes, or till partially set (consistency of unbeaten egg whites), stirring frequently. Or, transfer gelatin mixture to a bowl; chill about 1 hour, or till partially set, stirring occasionally (start watching mixture closely after 40 minutes).

■ Meanwhile, in a small mixing bowl combine cream cheese spread, powdered sugar, and vanilla. Beat with an electric mixer on medium speed till smooth. Spread mixture over bottom of cooled crust. Spoon *half* of the gelatin mixture over cream cheese layer. Top with *half* of the blackberries, all the raspberries, and then the remaining blackberries. Spoon the remaining gelatin mixture over the berries. Chill tart for 4 to 6 hours, or till set. To serve, loosen crust from sides of pan with a narrow spatula; remove the sides of the pan.

Makes 12 to 16 servings

Per serving: 250 calories, 3 g protein, 27 g carbohydrate, 15 g total fat (6 g saturated), 25 mg cholesterol, 191 mg sodium, 227 mg potassium

STEPS FOR COOLING GELATIN

STEP 1 **COOLING GELATIN OVER ICE BATH**
In a saucepan, stir together the gelatin and cherry juice. Let sit 5 minutes to soften the gelatin. Cook over low heat, stirring, until the gelatin dissolves. Remove from heat and set the saucepan in a large bowl of ice water.

STEP 2 **CHECKING GELATIN CONSISTENCY**
As the gelatin chills, it will begin to thicken. Stir often until the mixture is partially set (it will have the consistency of unbeaten egg whites). This should take about 15 minutes. Add more ice to bowl, if necessary, to maintain a cold temperature.

European styling and American
flavors come together in this col-
orful cross between a cheesecake
and a tart.

69

Crème Brûlée Tart

This elegant dessert presents an intriguing contrast in flavor and texture. The crisp crust holds a rich, creamy custard topped with a hot, sugary glaze. Unlike traditional crème brûlée, this topping also includes finely chopped nuts.

■ For pastry, in a medium mixing bowl, cut butter into flour till pieces are size of small peas. In a small mixing bowl combine egg yolk and *1 tablespoon* of the water. Gradually stir egg yolk mixture into flour mixture. Add remaining water, 1 tablespoon at a time, till dough is moistened. Gently knead dough just till a ball forms. For easier handling, cover with plastic wrap and chill for 30 to 60 minutes.

■ On a lightly floured surface, use your hands to slightly flatten the dough. Roll dough into an 11-inch circle. Ease pastry into a 9-inch tart pan; trim pastry even with the edge of the pan. Line *unpricked* pastry shell with a double thickness of foil. Bake in a preheated 375° oven for 10 minutes. Remove foil, brush crust with egg white, and bake 10 minutes more.

■ Meanwhile, for filling, in a large mixing bowl use a rotary beater or wire whisk to lightly beat eggs just till mixed. Stir in the granulated sugar and vanilla. Gradually stir in half-and-half, cream, or milk. With the pastry shell on the oven rack, pour the filling into the pastry shell. Reduce oven temperature to 350°. Bake for 25 to 35 minutes, or till a knife inserted near center comes out clean. Cool completely on a rack. Cover and chill for 2 to 24 hours before serving.

■ For brûlée topping, just before serving, press brown sugar through a sieve evenly over filling. Sprinkle with nuts. Broil 4 to 5 inches from the heat for 2 to 3 minutes, or till brown sugar begins to melt. Carefully remove sides of tart pan.

Makes 8 to 12 servings

Per serving: 320 calories, 6 g protein, 31 g carbohydrate, 19 g total fat (12 g saturated), 143 mg cholesterol, 183 mg sodium, 136 mg potassium

Preparation Time: 45 minutes
Baking Time: 45 to 55 minutes
Chilling Time: 2 to 24 hours
Broiling Time: 2 to 3 minutes

INGREDIENTS

PASTRY

1/2	CUP COLD BUTTER
1-1/4	CUPS ALL-PURPOSE FLOUR
1	BEATEN EGG YOLK
2 TO 3	TABLESPOONS WATER
1	SLIGHTLY BEATEN EGG WHITE

FILLING

3	EGGS
1/3	CUP GRANULATED SUGAR
1	TEASPOON VANILLA
1-1/4	CUPS HALF-AND-HALF, LIGHT CREAM, *OR* MILK

BRÛLÉE TOPPING

1/4	CUP PACKED BROWN SUGAR
2	TABLESPOONS FINELY CHOPPED PECANS

STEPS FOR MAKING BRÛLÉE TOPPING

STEP 1 PRESSING THE SUGAR

With a wooden spoon, press the packed brown sugar through a wire sieve held over the baked, cooled tart. Sprinkle with chopped pecans. Cover the custard evenly, or the topping will be too thick in spots.

STEP 2 TESTING FOR DONENESS

Broil 4 to 5 inches from the heat to melt the sugar and brown the nuts. The sugar will form a golden brown, textured surface on the custard, but as this is not a classic crème brûlée, it won't harden completely.

Choose this rich tart for special occasions. The topping is caramelized just before serving.

71

Black Bottom–Java Cream Tart

Preparation Time: 45 minutes
Baking Time: 15 to 20 minutes
Cooking Time: 15 minutes
Chilling Time: 4 to 24 hours

INGREDIENTS

TART PASTRY (PAGE 64)
1/3 CUP SEMISWEET CHOCOLATE PIECES *OR* CHOPPED SEMISWEET CHOCOLATE
1 TABLESPOON MARGARINE *OR* BUTTER
1/4 CUP WHIPPING CREAM
1 TEASPOON LIGHT CORN SYRUP
3/4 CUP SUGAR
3 TABLESPOONS CORNSTARCH
2 TEASPOONS INSTANT COFFEE CRYSTALS
1-3/4 CUPS MILK
2 BEATEN EGG YOLKS
1/2 CUP SEMISWEET CHOCOLATE PIECES *OR* CHOPPED SEMISWEET CHOCOLATE
2 TABLESPOONS MARGARINE *OR* BUTTER
1/2 TEASPOON VANILLA
1/2 CUP WHIPPING CREAM, WHIPPED
CHOCOLATE CURLS

*C*hocolate curls look lovely on this pie, but if you want a simpler decoration, sprinkle with grated chocolate or garnish with chocolate espresso beans. The fancy piped cream may be replaced with dollops spread evenly over the pie top.

■ Prepare pastry as directed. On a lightly floured surface, roll dough into a 13-inch circle. Ease pastry into an 11-inch tart pan with a removable bottom. Press pastry into fluted sides of tart pan; trim pastry even with the edge of the tart pan. Prick pastry. Line pastry with a double thickness of foil. Bake in a preheated 375° oven for 10 minutes. Remove foil and bake for 5 to 10 minutes more, or till light brown. Cool in pan on a rack.

■ Meanwhile, in a small heavy saucepan melt ⅓ cup chocolate pieces or chopped chocolate and 1 tablespoon margarine or butter over low heat; set aside. In a heavy saucepan stir together ¼ cup whipping cream and corn syrup. Bring to a gentle boil. Reduce heat and cook for 2 minutes. Remove from heat; stir in chocolate mixture. Cool to room temperature. Spread cooled mixture over the bottom and up the sides of the pastry shell; set aside.

■ In a medium saucepan combine sugar, cornstarch, and coffee crystals. Stir in milk. Cook and stir over medium heat till mixture is thickened and bubbly. Cook and stir for 2 minutes more. Remove from heat. Gradually stir about *half* of the hot mixture into the beaten egg yolks. Return all to saucepan. Cook and stir till bubbly. Reduce heat. Cook and stir for 2 minutes more. Remove from heat. Stir in ½ cup chocolate pieces or chopped chocolate, 2 tablespoons margarine or butter, and the vanilla till chocolate is melted. Pour into pastry shell. Cover surface with plastic wrap. Chill for 4 to 24 hours, or till firm. To serve, carefully remove plastic wrap; remove sides of pan. Pipe whipped cream over top of pie. Garnish with chocolate curls.

Makes 8 servings

Per serving: 527 calories, 7 g protein, 57 g carbohydrate, 33 g total fat (17 g saturated), 172 mg cholesterol, 225 mg sodium, 206 mg potassium

STEPS FOR MAKING CHOCOLATE CURLS AND PIPING CREAM

STEP 1 **MAKING CURLS**

It's important that the chocolate be at room temperature in order to make curls. To soften cold chocolate, hold it in your hand briefly to warm or let it stand at room temperature. Then, holding the block in one hand, pull across the chocolate in an easy motion with a vegetable peeler, letting the curls drop onto a piece of waxed paper or a chilled plate below.

STEP 2 FILLING A PASTRY BAG

Whip the cream to stiff peaks. Set a pastry bag fitted with a decorative tip in a measuring cup. Fold down the top of the bag to form a collar. With a rubber spatula or a spoon, fill the pastry bag with whipped cream. Unfold the collar and twist the bag just above the filling. Squeeze the bag to push out excess air.

STEP 3 PIPING THE CREAM

With one hand, grasp the pastry bag around the twisted closure. Set the other hand under the bag close to the tip. Pipe by squeezing with a continual, even pressure at the top of the bag and guiding from the bottom.

To make star-shaped decorations, pipe whipped cream straight down onto the surface of the pie, lifting straight up after each squeeze. To make lines of cream, pipe at an angle, squeezing out the cream gently as you go. Sprinkle chocolate curls over cream.

Glazed Applecot Tart

*D*ried *fruits have an intense, concentrated flavor, so you'll want to serve small pieces of this dense tart. A scoop of ice cream will complement it perfectly.*

■ In a large saucepan, combine water, dried apples, and dried apricots. Bring to boiling; reduce heat. Cover and simmer for 5 minutes. Drain. In a medium mixing bowl combine brown sugar and cornstarch. Stir in almonds, ⅓ cup apricot nectar or orange juice, the cinnamon, nutmeg, and fruit. Set mixture aside.

■ Prepare pastry as directed. On a lightly floured surface, roll dough into a 13-inch square or circle. Ease pastry into a square or round 11-inch tart pan with a removable bottom. Press pastry into fluted sides of tart pan; trim pastry even with the edge of the tart pan. Transfer filling to pastry-lined tart pan. Bake in a preheated 375° oven for 40 minutes.

■ In a small bowl combine apricot preserves and the 1 tablespoon apricot nectar or orange juice. Brush over top of warm tart. Cool on a rack. To serve, remove sides of tart pan. If desired, serve with ice cream.

Makes 10 servings

Per serving: 368 calories, 4 g protein, 62 g carbohydrate, 13 g total fat (8 g saturated), 68 mg cholesterol, 134 mg sodium, 446 mg potassium

For a glistening appearance, brush this dried-fruit tart with an apricot glaze after it comes out of the oven.

INGREDIENTS

3	CUPS WATER
1	6-OUNCE PACKAGE DRIED APPLES
1	6-OUNCE PACKAGE DRIED APRICOTS, HALVED
3/4	CUP PACKED BROWN SUGAR
1	TABLESPOON CORNSTARCH
1/2	CUP CHOPPED ALMONDS
1/3	CUP APRICOT NECTAR *OR* ORANGE JUICE
1/8	TEASPOON GROUND CINNAMON
1/8	TEASPOON GROUND NUTMEG
	TART PASTRY (PAGE 64)
1/4	CUP APRICOT PRESERVES
1	TABLESPOON APRICOT NECTAR *OR* ORANGE JUICE
	ICE CREAM (OPTIONAL)

Preparation Time: 35 minutes
Cooking Time: 5 minutes
Baking Time: 40 minutes

STEPS AT A GLANCE	Page
MAKING TARTS	64

74

Honey & Nut Tart

INGREDIENTS

Preparation Time: 40 minutes
Baking Time: 40 to 50 minutes

PASTRY

	PASTRY FOR SINGLE-CRUST PIE (PAGE 14)
1/4	CUP GROUND PECANS *OR* WALNUTS

FILLING

2	EGGS
1/2	CUP PACKED BROWN SUGAR
1/2	CUP HONEY
3	TABLESPOONS MARGARINE *OR* BUTTER, MELTED
1/4	TEASPOON FINELY SHREDDED ORANGE PEEL
2	TEASPOONS ORANGE LIQUEUR (OPTIONAL)
1	CUP COARSELY CHOPPED SALTED MIXED COCKTAIL NUTS *OR* COARSELY CHOPPED NUTS SUCH AS PEANUTS, PECANS, HAZELNUTS, AND/OR WALNUTS

ORANGE WHIPPED CREAM

1/2	CUP WHIPPING CREAM
2	TABLESPOONS POWDERED SUGAR
2	TEASPOONS ORANGE LIQUEUR

*M*ixed nuts team with a honey and brown sugar base to make a tart that tastes similar to a pecan pie. Additional nuts blended into the pastry carry on the theme.

■ Prepare pastry as directed, stirring ground pecans or walnuts into the flour mixture before adding water. On a lightly floured surface, roll dough into a 13-inch circle. Ease pastry into an 11-inch tart pan with a removable bottom. Press pastry into fluted sides of tart pan; trim pastry even with the edge of the tart pan. Prick pastry. Line pastry shell with a double thickness of foil. Bake in a preheated 375° oven for 10 minutes. Remove foil and bake for 5 to 10 minutes more, or till pastry is light brown. Cool pastry in pan on a rack. Reduce oven temperature to 350°.

■ For filling, in a medium mixing bowl use a rotary beater or wire whisk to lightly beat eggs. Stir in brown sugar, honey, margarine or butter, orange peel, and, if desired, orange liqueur. Mix well. Stir in mixed nuts. Pour the filling into the pastry shell. Bake in the 350° oven for 25 to 30 minutes, or till center is just set. Cool on a rack.

■ For orange whipped cream, beat whipping cream, powdered sugar, and orange liqueur together till soft peaks form. Serve immediately with the tart.

Makes 10 to 12 servings

Per serving: 410 calories, 6 g protein, 42 g carbohydrate, 26 g total fat (7 g saturated), 59 mg cholesterol, 117 mg sodium, 180 mg potassium

Decorate this nut tart with orange-flavored whipped cream and a spiral of orange peel.

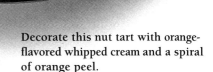

STEPS AT A GLANCE	**Page**
MAKING TARTS	64

Lemon Curd–Raspberry Tartlets

Preparation Time: 1 hour
Baking Time: 5 to 8 minutes
Cooking Time: 8 minutes
Chilling Time (optional): 24 hours

STEPS AT A GLANCE	Page
MAKING TARTLETS	66

INGREDIENTS

TART PASTRY (PAGE 64)

LEMON CURD

1/2 CUP SUGAR

4 TEASPOONS CORNSTARCH

1 TEASPOON FINELY SHREDDED
   LEMON PEEL

3/4 CUP WATER

2 BEATEN EGG YOLKS

1/4 CUP LEMON JUICE

2 TABLESPOONS MARGARINE
   OR BUTTER

GARNISH

24 RASPBERRIES

24 FRESH MINT SPRIGS (OPTIONAL)

*T*he wonderful flavor of the lemon curd also enhances other seasonal fruits such as sweet cherry halves, strawberry, apricot, or plum slices, or kiwifruit wedges.

■ Prepare pastry as directed and shape into twenty-four ¾-inch balls. Press balls into ungreased 1¾-inch mini muffin cups, pressing an even layer onto the bottom and up the sides of each cup. Bake in a preheated 450° oven for 5 to 8 minutes, or till edges are light brown. Completely cool pastry shells in muffin cups on a rack. Remove pastry shells from muffin cups and set aside.

■ Meanwhile, for lemon curd, in a small saucepan combine sugar, cornstarch, and lemon peel. Stir in water. Cook and stir till thickened and bubbly. Gradually stir about *½ cup* of the hot mixture into egg yolks; return all to saucepan. Cook and stir over medium heat till mixture boils. Cook and stir 2 minutes more. Remove from heat. Stir in lemon juice and margarine or butter, stirring till margarine or butter melts. Spoon about *2 teaspoons* of the lemon curd into each pastry shell. Place on a platter. If desired, cover and chill tartlets for up to 24 hours. Just before serving, place a raspberry and, if desired, a sprig of mint on each tartlet.

Makes 24 tartlets

Per serving: 100 calories, 1 g protein, 12 g carbohydrate, 6 g total fat (3 g saturated), 46 mg cholesterol, 51 mg sodium, 19 mg potassium

Guests will devour these jewel-like tartlets in one bite. Try to find the tiniest mint sprigs you can to place on each tartlet.

Orange-glazed Fruit Tartlets

As a handy shortcut, this fruit filling is cooked in a glaze rather than painted with it after baking.

STEPS AT A GLANCE	Page
MAKING TARTLETS	66

Preparation Time: 35 minutes
Baking Time: 10 to 12 minutes
Cooking Time: 4 minutes
Chilling Time (optional): 2 hours

INGREDIENTS

	TART PASTRY (PAGE 64)
1/4	CUP SUGAR
2	TEASPOONS CORNSTARCH
1/2	CUP ORANGE JUICE
3	CUPS FRESH FRUIT, SUCH AS SLICED STRAWBERRIES, SLICED PEELED PEACHES OR NECTARINES, HALVED GRAPES, RASPBERRIES, OR BLUEBERRIES

77

*T*hese tartlets can also be made in 2½-inch muffin pans if you divide the dough into 12 portions and roll each portion into a 4-inch circle to line the cups. Bake them for about 12 minutes.

■ Prepare pastry as directed and divide into 8 portions. On a lightly floured surface, use your hands to slightly flatten the dough. Roll each dough portion into a 5-inch circle. Carefully line eight 3- to 3½-inch fluted tartlet pans with pastry. Trim pastry even with the edge of each tartlet pan. Prick bottoms and sides of pastry with the tines of a fork. Place tartlet pans on a baking sheet. Bake in a preheated 375° oven for 10 to 12 minutes, or till light brown. Cool several minutes, then remove from pans. Cool shells completely on a rack.

■ Meanwhile, in a medium saucepan stir together sugar and cornstarch. Stir in orange juice. Cook and stir over medium heat till thickened and bubbly. Cook and stir for 2 minutes more. Gently stir in fruit. Divide fruit mixture evenly among the baked pastry shells. If desired, chill for up to 2 hours.

Makes 8 servings

Per serving: 257 calories, 3 g protein, 33 g carbohydrate, 13 g total fat (8 g saturated), 84 mg cholesterol, 119 mg sodium, 154 mg potassium

White Mousse Tart with Raspberry Sauce

Preparation Time: 1 hour
Baking Time: 12 to 15 minutes
Cooking Time: 8 minutes
Chilling Time: 4 to 24 hours

INGREDIENTS

CHOCOLATE PASTRY

1-1/4	CUPS ALL-PURPOSE FLOUR
2	TABLESPOONS SUGAR
2	TABLESPOONS UNSWEETENED COCOA POWDER
1/4	TEASPOON SALT
1/2	CUP SHORTENING *OR* BUTTER
4	TO 5 TABLESPOONS WATER

FILLING

1/2	CUP SUGAR
1	ENVELOPE UNFLAVORED GELATIN
1-1/3	CUPS MILK
3	SLIGHTLY BEATEN EGG YOLKS
1	6-OUNCE PACKAGE WHITE BAKING BAR, CHOPPED
1/2	CUP WHIPPING CREAM

RASPBERRY SAUCE

1	10-OUNCE PACKAGE FROZEN SWEETENED RED RASPBERRIES (IN QUICK-THAW POUCH)
	WATER
1	TABLESPOON CORNSTARCH
1/3	CUP CURRANT JELLY

*L*ook for the white baking bar in the same section as the baking chocolate at your supermarket. Not strictly chocolate, it is made of cocoa butter with sugar, milk solids, and flavorings. Serve the raspberry sauce alongside the tart or spooned over each slice.

■ For chocolate pastry, in a medium bowl stir together flour, sugar, cocoa powder, and salt. Cut in shortening or butter till pieces are the size of small peas. Sprinkle water, 1 tablespoon at a time, over dough, tossing with a fork till all is moistened. Form dough into a ball. On a lightly floured surface, roll dough into a 13-inch circle. Ease pastry into an 11-inch tart pan with a removable bottom. Press pastry into fluted sides of tart pan; trim pastry even with the edge of the tart pan. Line *unpricked* pastry shell with a double thickness of foil. Bake in a preheated 450° oven for 12 to 15 minutes, or till pastry is set and dry. Cool on a rack.

■ For filling, in a medium saucepan combine sugar and gelatin. Stir in milk and egg yolks. Cook and stir over medium heat till gelatin dissolves and mixture thickens slightly and just begins to bubble. Stir in chopped white baking bar just till melted. Set the saucepan in a large bowl of ice water for about 15 minutes, or till partially set (consistency of corn syrup), stirring frequently. Or, transfer gelatin mixture to a bowl; chill about 1 hour, or till partially set, stirring occasionally (start watching mixture closely after 40 minutes). Beat whipping cream till soft peaks form (tips curl); fold whipped cream into gelatin mixture. Transfer filling to cooled pastry shell. Chill for 4 to 24 hours, or till firm.

■ For raspberry sauce, thaw raspberries. Drain raspberries, reserving syrup. Add water to syrup to equal ¾ cup. In a small saucepan combine syrup mixture and cornstarch. Stir in currant jelly. Cook and stir over medium heat till thickened and bubbly. Cook and stir for 2 minutes more. Stir in raspberries. Chill well, then serve with the tart.

Makes 8 servings

Per serving: 530 calories, 7 g protein, 65 g carbohydrate, 28 g total fat (12 g saturated), 104 mg cholesterol, 123 mg sodium, 239 mg potassium

Snow white wedges of this chilled tart look spectacular when dressed with a ribbon of raspberry sauce and a sprig of fresh mint.

Pastry Wraps

Steps for Making Dumplings

ROLLING PIN

BASIC TOOLS FOR MAKING DUMPLINGS

Dumplings require rolling and cutting tools, plus a cake pan "template" and a pastry brush and bowl for water.

SMALL BOWL AND
PASTRY BRUSH

PARING KNIFE

FLUTED PASTRY WHEEL

80

8-INCH ROUND CAKE PAN
AND CUTTING BOARD

Dumplings and turnovers are essentially pies with a difference. A dumpling is a whole fruit encased in pastry, while a turnover encloses a sweet or savory filling that can be a single ingredient or several. Basic pie pastry provides the foundation for both. The dough is rolled out and cut into portions, then either wrapped or folded around the filling.

Both dumplings and turnovers have homespun reputations. The Shakers, an American religious sect known for their good, plain food, favored pastry-wrapped fruit dumplings drenched in maple syrup, while Cornish miners carried meat-and-vegetable-filled turnovers called pasties in their lunch pails.

Although sometimes viewed as old-fashioned country fare, dumplings and turnovers can be dressed up with the simple addition of decorations created out of dough scraps. The charming leaves on Pastry-wrapped Pears and Apple Dumplings, opposite, are two fine examples. More about turnovers on the following pages.

some recipes may call for you to cut the dough into a square; if so, use a ruler to mark off the lines

STEP 1 CUTTING A CIRCLE OF DOUGH

For each dumpling, roll out 1 ball of dough into a thick, flat disc. Place an 8-inch cake pan or plate atop the dough and cut around it to make an 8-inch circle of dough.

leave an opening at the top of the dough so steam can escape as the apple bakes

pink the ends of each strip on the diagonal so it looks more decorative

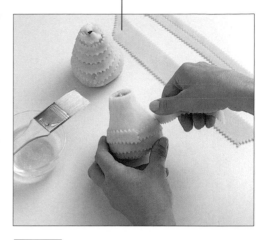

STEP 2 **WRAPPING FRUIT WITH PASTRY**

To wrap an apple or other spherical fruit, set the filled fruit in the center of the pastry circle. Lift dough up around fruit, easing in excess dough around the stem end by gathering it in small pleats. Gently press down on each pleat to seal.

STEP 3 **ATTACHING DECORATIONS**

With a small knife, cut leaves freehand from the pastry scraps. Brush the underside of each leaf with water, then gently attach it to the top of the dumpling, pressing lightly to adhere.

STEP 4 **WRAPPING FRUIT WITH STRIPS**

To wrap elongated fruits such as pears, first cut strips of dough with a pastry wheel. Starting at the edge of the curved bottom of the pear, attach a strip and wind it around, overlapping the edges. Brush the end of a second strip with water, overlap it on the first, then wrap it around; repeat with the third strip.

81

make a "central" vein, then branch out smaller veins diagonally

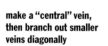

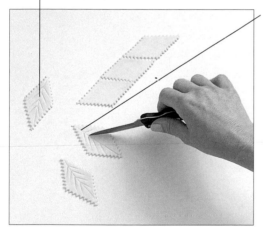

when making the veins, don't press all the way through the dough

STEP 5 **CREATING DIAMOND LEAVES**

Cut a 1½-inch strip of dough on the diagonal with a fluted pastry wheel to make diamond-shaped leaves. "Draw" veins by pressing lines into the leaves with the back of a knife. Attach as directed in step 3.

Apple and pear dumplings are beautifully decorated with pastry leaves. The recipe for Pastry-wrapped Stuffed Pears is on page 85, while Apple Dumplings is on page 86.

Steps for Making Turnovers

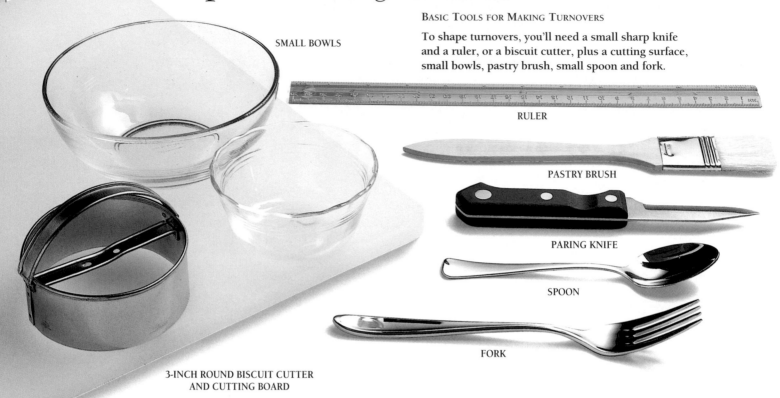

SMALL BOWLS

BASIC TOOLS FOR MAKING TURNOVERS

To shape turnovers, you'll need a small sharp knife and a ruler, or a biscuit cutter, plus a cutting surface, small bowls, pastry brush, small spoon and fork.

RULER

PASTRY BRUSH

PARING KNIFE

SPOON

FORK

3-INCH ROUND BISCUIT CUTTER
AND CUTTING BOARD

ALTHOUGH MADE WITH pie pastry, a turnover doesn't require a special pan to shape it. In most cases, except when cut from a certain pattern such as the pastry-wrapped salmon on page 88, it actually shapes itself. Fold a square of dough in half crosswise and it becomes a rectangle; fold it on the diagonal and you have a triangle. A half-moon is made by folding a circle in half, while a fan is a half-moon set upright on its folded edge.

Like dumplings, most turnovers are a single serving, a plus for entertaining because you know exactly how many portions you will get from any one recipe. On the other hand, some of the most elegant main courses consist of meat or fish wrapped *en croûte* — in a pastry case — sized large enough to serve as many as six people. Small turnovers are perfectly sized for out-of-hand hors d'oeuvres.

Best of all, the versatile turnover couldn't be easier to assemble: Simply roll, fill, seal, and bake!

if you don't have a biscuit cutter, use a plastic lid as a template and cut around it with a knife

STEP 1 CUTTING SQUARES OR CIRCLES

With a small, sharp knife and a ruler as a guide, or with a floured round biscuit cutter, cut the pastry into squares or circles as directed in the recipe.

don't put too much
filling on the dough,
or it will leak out onto
the baking sheet

83

STEP 2 SPOONING ON FILLING

Spread the filling in a rough triangle over half of the dough square. For a circle, arrange the filling in a half-moon shape. Leave a ½-inch border around the filling so the turnover can be sealed after it is folded.

The whimsical patterns on the tops and edges of these very appealing turnovers were easily created with a fork, knife, or toothpick.

as you seal the turnover, you
push out air so the pastry
doesn't pop open as it bakes

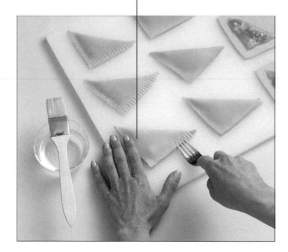

you can also
create vents by
piercing the
dough with a
toothpick in a
dotted pattern

STEP 3 SEALING TURNOVERS

Moisten the edge of the turnover with water, using a small pastry brush or a dampened finger. Fold the pastry in half. Seal by pressing the edge with the tines of a fork, working from each end to the center point.

STEP 4 VENTING TURNOVERS

Now that the pastry is sealed, an opening must be made somewhere on the top surface to allow steam to escape during baking. With a small, sharp knife, make several slits near the folded edge of the pastry.

84

Encased in a spiral of pastry, baked pears take on a new elegance. Offer with half-and-half or light cream alongside to pour over each serving.

Pastry-wrapped Stuffed Pears

Preparation Time: 45 minutes
Baking Time: 40 to 45 minutes

INGREDIENTS

1/4	CUP ORANGE MARMALADE
2	TABLESPOONS CHOPPED WALNUTS
4	SMALL PEARS
	PASTRY FOR SINGLE-CRUST PIE (PAGE 14)
4	WHOLE CLOVES
1	EGG WHITE
1	TABLESPOON WATER
1	TABLESPOON SUGAR
	HALF-AND-HALF *OR* LIGHT CREAM

Tawny, slender Bosc pears or golden Bartletts work best for this recipe. Be sure to choose small pears with stable bottoms so they can stand on end during baking.

■ In a small mixing bowl combine orange marmalade and walnuts. Set aside. Peel and core pears, leaving bottoms intact. Spoon filling into the center of each pear.

■ Prepare pastry as directed, *except* roll dough into a 13-inch square. Trim pastry to form a 12-inch square. Use a fluted pastry wheel or knife to cut dough into twelve 12x¾-inch-wide strips and one 1½-inch-wide strip. Pat pears with paper towels. Using one of the pastry strips and starting ½ inch above the base of a pear (do not cover bottom of pear), wrap pastry strip around pear. Moisten end of strip and seal to the end of a second pastry strip. Complete wrapping pear with third pastry strip to cover the hole and filling. Moisten end to seal. Repeat, using 3 pastry strips on each remaining pear.

■ With a knife or cookie cutter, cut leaf shapes from 1½-inch-wide pastry strips; mark veins on leaves. Moisten leaves and attach to tops of pears. Top pears with whole cloves for stems. Stir together egg white and water; brush onto pastry. Sprinkle with sugar. Transfer pears to a shallow baking dish. Bake in a preheated 400° oven for 40 to 45 minutes, or till golden. Serve warm with half-and-half or light cream.

Makes 4 servings

Per serving: 454 calories, 6 g protein, 62 g carbohydrate, 22 g total fat (6 g saturated), 5 mg cholesterol, 158 mg sodium, 228 mg potassium

STEPS AT A GLANCE	Page
STUFFING PEARS	85
MAKING DOUGH	8
MAKING DUMPLINGS	80

85

STEPS FOR STUFFING PEARS

STEP 1 CORING PEARS

Slice off a little of the neck of each pear to make a flat surface. Insert a corer about three fourths of the way into the pear and twist, then remove and discard the core.

STEP 2 FILLING PEARS

You will need to use a very small spoon to fill the pears, as the opening is narrow. A baby spoon or iced-tea spoon is a good size if you have one. Spoon the filling into each pear just to the top. Don't overfill or the dumplings will take too long to bake through.

Apple Dumplings

Preparation Time: 40 minutes
Cooking Time: 5 minutes
Baking Time: 45 minutes

STEPS AT A GLANCE	Page
MAKING DOUGH	8
MAKING DUMPLINGS	80
POURING SYRUP	86

For a sweet surprise, spoon raisins, dried cranberries, or dried cherries into the center of each apple before wrapping it with pastry.

■ For syrup, in a medium saucepan combine water, sugar, nutmeg, cinnamon and, if desired, food coloring. Bring to boiling. Reduce heat and simmer, uncovered, for 5 minutes. Remove from heat; stir in margarine or butter.

■ For dumplings, prepare pastry as directed, *except* divide dough into 4 equal portions. Form each into a ball. On a lightly floured surface, roll each portion of dough into a circle about ⅛ inch thick. Trim each portion to an 8-inch circle. Place 1 apple in center of each pastry circle. Combine the sugar, nutmeg, and cinnamon; sprinkle over fruit.

■ Moisten edge of pastry with water. Bring dough up around apple to resemble a bundle, pressing the edges together at the top to seal. Using a knife or small cookie cutter, cut leaf shapes from pastry scraps. Moisten bottom sides of pastry leaves with water and place leaves on top of the wrapped apples, gently pressing to seal.

■ Place wrapped apples in an ungreased 2-quart square baking dish. Pour syrup over dumplings. Bake in a pre-heated 375° oven about 45 minutes, or till apples are tender and pastry is golden. Serve warm with ice cream, if desired.

Makes 4 servings

Per serving: 697 calories, 6 g protein; 86 g carbohydrate, 38 g total fat (9 g saturated), 0 mg cholesterol, 305 mg sodium, 140 mg potassium

INGREDIENTS

SYRUP

1-2/3	CUPS WATER
1/2	CUP SUGAR
1/4	TEASPOON GROUND NUTMEG
1/4	TEASPOON GROUND CINNAMON
	FEW DROPS RED FOOD COLORING (OPTIONAL)
1	TABLESPOON MARGARINE OR BUTTER

DUMPLINGS

	PASTRY FOR DOUBLE-CRUST PIE (PAGE 14)
4	SMALL COOKING APPLES, PEELED AND CORED (ABOUT 4 OUNCES EACH)
2	TABLESPOONS SUGAR
1/8	TEASPOON GROUND NUTMEG
1/8	TEASPOON GROUND CINNAMON
	ICE CREAM (OPTIONAL)

STEP FOR POURING SYRUP

STEP 1 POURING SYRUP

The syrup will glaze the pastry and also serve as a sauce for the dumplings. Make the syrup by heating water, sugar, and spices in a saucepan; for a red tint, add food coloring. Remove from heat and stir in margarine or butter. Place the dumplings in a baking dish. Pour syrup over and around the dumplings, then bake.

Serve each dumpling with additional
sauce; spoon the sauce over the ice
cream if that is offered as well.

Salmon en Croûte with Chive Crème Fraîche

Preparation Time: 1 hour
Standing Time: 2 to 5 hours
Cooking Time: 9 minutes
Baking Time: 20 to 25 minutes

INGREDIENTS

CHIVE CRÈME FRAÎCHE

1/2	CUP WHIPPING CREAM (NOT ULTRA-PASTEURIZED)
1/2	CUP DAIRY SOUR CREAM
4	TEASPOONS SNIPPED FRESH CHIVES *OR* CHOPPED GREEN ONION TOPS

SALMON EN CROÛTE

1	10-OUNCE PACKAGE FROZEN CHOPPED SPINACH
1/2	CUP CHOPPED ONION
1	TABLESPOON MARGARINE *OR* BUTTER
1/4	CUP FINE DRY SEASONED BREAD CRUMBS
1	SLIGHTLY BEATEN EGG
1/2	TEASPOON FINELY SHREDDED LEMON PEEL
1/4	TEASPOON SALT
2	12-OUNCE SKINLESS SALMON FILLETS (3/4 TO 1 INCH THICK)
	PASTRY FOR DOUBLE-CRUST PIE (PAGE 14)
1	SLIGHTLY BEATEN EGG
1	TABLESPOON WATER

*I*f you don't have time to make the special crème fraîche, simply stir some snipped chives or dill into dairy sour cream or plain yogurt for a fine alternative.

■ For chive crème fraîche, in a mixing bowl stir together whipping cream and sour cream. Cover with plastic wrap. Let stand at room temperature for 2 to 5 hours, or till mixture thickens. When thickened, stir in chives, cover, and chill till serving time or for up to 1 week. Stir before serving.

■ For salmon en croûte, cook spinach according to package directions. Drain well, squeezing to remove excess liquid. In a medium saucepan cook onion in margarine or butter about 5 minutes or till tender but not brown. Stir in spinach, bread crumbs, 1 egg, lemon peel, and salt. Set aside. In a large skillet bring 2 cups *water* to boiling. Carefully add salmon. Return just to boiling. Reduce heat and simmer, covered, for 4 minutes. Remove fish; pat dry (fish will not be done). Sprinkle fish with a little additional salt.

■ Prepare pastry as directed and divide into 2 pieces, one piece about a third larger than the other. Lay fillets side by side with long sides just touching. Measure total length and width of fillets. On a lightly floured surface roll the smaller portion of pastry to a size about 2 inches longer and wider than the fish fillets. Transfer pastry to an ungreased baking sheet. Spread *half* of the filling to within 1 inch of the edges of pastry. Place fillets on top of filling, placing long sides together as directed above. Spread remaining filling evenly over both fillets. Roll out remaining pastry. Combine 1 egg and water; brush onto edges of bottom pastry. Place remaining pastry over fish and filling to cover. Evenly trim all edges, reserving scraps. (If desired, trim pastry to the shape of a large fish). Seal edges with the tines of a fork or crimp edges. Reroll scraps and cut into decorations, if desired. Brush the top of the crust with some remaining egg mixture, decorate with pastry cutouts, then brush cutouts with egg mixture; make slits in top of pastry. Bake in a preheated 400° oven for 20 to 25 minutes, or till internal temperature is 160°. Serve with chive crème fraîche.

Makes 6 servings

Per serving: 545 calories, 24 g protein, 31 g carbohydrate, 36 g total fat (13 g saturated), 127 mg cholesterol, 430 mg sodium, 412 mg potassium

STEPS FOR DECORATING FISH

STEP 1 **CUTTING OUT A FISH**

Use parchment paper or clean brown paper to make a pattern. Lay the pattern on the pastry and cut around it with a knife.

STEP 2 **MAKING FINS**

Reroll dough scraps and cut out pieces for fins. Brush with water and press onto the fish. Press into the cutouts with the back of a knife to make ridges.

STEP 3 **ADDING SCALES**

Use a half-moon–shaped hors d'oeuvre cutter with sharp edges. Make scales by pressing into the dough with the outward curving edge of the cutter; do not press through the dough.

88

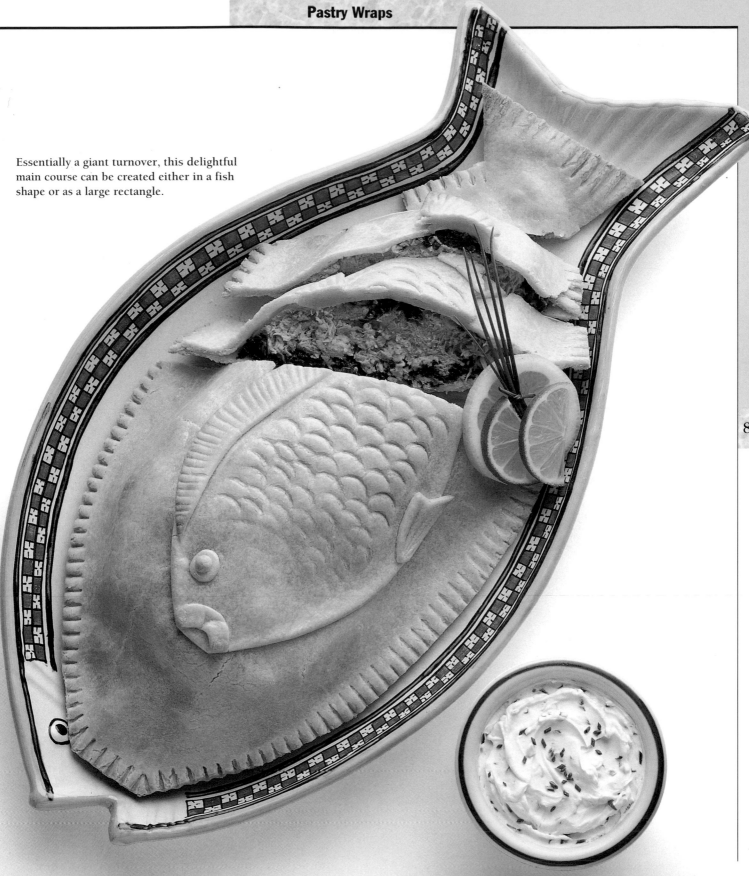

Essentially a giant turnover, this delightful main course can be created either in a fish shape or as a large rectangle.

89

Fresh and hot from the oven, these savory
bite-sized turnovers are dipped into a bowl
of warm tomato sauce to eat.

Zesty Italian Bites

STEPS AT A GLANCE	Page
MAKING DOUGH	8
MAKING TURNOVERS	82
PLEATING TURNOVERS	91

Preparation Time: 45 minutes
Cooking Time: 5 minutes
Baking Time: 15 to 20 minutes

INGREDIENTS

PASTRY

2	CUPS ALL-PURPOSE FLOUR
1/4	TEASPOON SALT
1/4	CUP SHORTENING
1/4	CUP COLD BUTTER
1	EGG YOLK
1/3	CUP COLD WATER

FILLING AND SAUCE

6	OUNCES BULK SWEET ITALIAN SAUSAGE OR SAUSAGE LINKS (CASINGS REMOVED)
1/4	CUP FINELY CHOPPED ONION
3	OUNCES MOZZARELLA CHEESE, SHREDDED (3/4 CUP)
2	TABLESPOONS GRATED PARMESAN CHEESE
	BOTTLED OR HOMEMADE SPAGHETTI SAUCE

*G*ive these turnovers a festive look by pleating the edges *and baking them upright. The folding technique is the same as for a Chinese potsticker, which these resemble.*

■ For pastry, in a medium mixing bowl combine flour and salt. Cut in shortening and butter till mixture resembles coarse crumbs. Make a well in the center. Beat together egg yolk and water; add to flour mixture. Stir till moistened. Form dough into a ball; divide dough in half. Wrap each half of dough in plastic wrap; chill in the freezer for 20 minutes. Meanwhile, for filling, cook sausage and onion till sausage is brown and onion is tender. Drain well; cool completely. Stir in mozzarella cheese and Parmesan.

■ On a lightly floured surface, roll each half of dough to slightly less than ⅛-inch thickness. Cut dough into rounds with a floured 4-inch round cutter. Spoon about *1 rounded teaspoon* of the filling onto the center of each circle. Brush edge with water. Fold dough over filling; pinch edges to pleat. Repeat with remaining dough and filling. Cut several small slits near edge of each turnover. Set folded edge upright; press down gently to slightly flatten the bottoms. Place on a large ungreased baking sheet. Bake in a preheated 375° oven for 15 to 20 minutes, or till golden. For sauce, warm spaghetti sauce and serve in a bowl alongside for dipping.

Makes about 24 to 30 appetizers

Per serving: 111 calories, 3 g protein, 9 g carbohydrate, 7 g total fat (3 g saturated), 20 mg cholesterol, 177 mg sodium, 77 mg potassium

91

STEPS FOR PLEATING TURNOVERS

STEP 1 MOISTENING EDGES
Spoon the filling onto the center of each 4-inch round of dough. Brush bare edge of the dough with water.

STEP 2 FOLDING TURNOVERS
Be sure that there is a border of dough all around the filling. Pick up the turnover with your hands and fold it in half, but don't press it together.

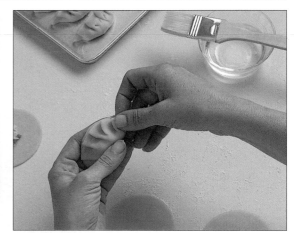

STEP 3 PLEATING TURNOVERS
On the top half of the turnover, gather the edge of the dough closest to you into small pleats, working from right to left. Pinch gently to seal.

Nectarine Dumplings with Ginger Syrup

Preparation Time: 35 minutes
Baking Time: 35 to 40 minutes
Cooking Time: 15 to 20 minutes

INGREDIENTS

DUMPLINGS

2	TABLESPOONS SNIPPED CHUTNEY
2	TABLESPOONS CHOPPED PECANS
1	TABLESPOON RAISINS
	PASTRY FOR SINGLE-CRUST PIE (PAGE 14)
4	MEDIUM NECTARINES, PEELED, HALVED, AND PITTED
1	EGG WHITE
1	TABLESPOON WATER
	SUGAR

GINGER SYRUP

1-1/4	CUPS WATER
3/4	CUP PACKED BROWN SUGAR
1	TABLESPOON LEMON JUICE
1/2	TEASPOON GROUND GINGER
2	TABLESPOONS MARGARINE OR BUTTER

*C*hutney is a spicy, sweet relish made from fruits and/or vegetables; the most well known is mango chutney. It usually contains some large chunks that will need to be chopped or snipped with scissors for this recipe.

■ For dumplings, in a small mixing bowl combine chutney, pecans, and raisins; set aside. Prepare pastry as directed, *except* roll pastry into a 14-inch square. Cut the pastry into four 7-inch squares. Place 1 nectarine half, cut side up, on the center of each pastry square. Spoon filling mixture onto centers of fruit. Place remaining fruit halves on top of filled fruit. Moisten edges of pastry with water. Fold corners to center on top of fruit, pinching edges together to seal. Place in a lightly greased 2-quart square baking dish. In a small bowl beat together egg white and water. Brush dumplings with egg white mixture. Sprinkle with sugar. Bake in a preheated 400° oven for 35 to 40 minutes, or till golden.

■ Meanwhile, for ginger syrup, in a medium saucepan combine water, brown sugar, lemon juice, and ginger. Bring to boiling. Reduce heat and simmer, uncovered, for 15 to 20 minutes or till syruplike. Remove from heat; stir in margarine or butter. Serve with dumplings.

Makes 4 servings

Per serving: 467 calories, 6 g protein, 55 g carbohydrate, 26 g total fat (6 g saturated), 0 mg cholesterol, 220 mg sodium, 387 mg potassium

Twist the corners of each pastry square together at the center to give the appearance of a topknot.

92

Plum Dumplings

Preparation Time: 20 minutes
Baking Time: 30 minutes

INGREDIENTS

1/4	CUP SUGAR
1/4	TEASPOON GROUND NUTMEG
1/2	OF A 3-OUNCE PACKAGE CREAM CHEESE, SOFTENED
	TART PASTRY (PAGE 64)
6	PLUMS, HALVED AND PITTED
	HALF-AND-HALF OR LIGHT CREAM

*S*imple, yet impressive, this recipe is also *delicious made with small nectarines or peeled peaches in place of the plums.*

■ In a small mixing bowl stir together sugar and nutmeg. Set aside. In another small mixing bowl beat cream cheese with an electric mixer on medium speed till fluffy. Add 3 *tablespoons* of the sugar-nutmeg mixture. Beat till well combined. Set aside.

■ Prepare pastry as directed. On a lightly floured surface roll dough into an 18x12-inch rectangle. Cut into six 6-inch squares. For each dumpling, spread 2 *teaspoons* of the cream cheese mixture on the cut side of a plum half. Top with another plum half. Place in the center of a dough square. Moisten dough edges with water. Fold corners to center and pinch to seal edges.

■ Place the dumplings in a shallow baking pan. Brush with some of the half-and-half or light cream and sprinkle with the remaining sugar-nutmeg mixture. Bake dumplings in a preheated 375° oven about 30 minutes, or till plums are tender and pastry is golden. Serve warm with half-and-half or light cream.

Makes 6 servings

Per serving: 361 calories, 5 g protein, 39 g carbohydrate, 21 g fat (13 g saturated), 59 mg cholesterol, 273 mg sodium, 177 mg potassium

Cut into a freshly baked plum dumpling, then pour in a bit of half-and-half or light cream for cool contrast.

Apricot–Cream Cheese Turnovers

STEPS AT A GLANCE	Page
MAKING DOUGH	8
MAKING TURNOVERS	82

Preparation Time: 30 minutes
Baking Time: 15 to 20 minutes

INGREDIENTS

	PASTRY FOR DOUBLE-CRUST PIE (PAGE 14)
1	3-OUNCE PACKAGE CREAM CHEESE, SOFTENED
1	EGG YOLK
1/3	CUP APRICOT *OR* PEACH PRESERVES
1	CUP SIFTED POWDERED SUGAR
1/4	TEASPOON VANILLA
1	TO 2 TABLESPOONS MILK

Like a cheesecake wrapped in pastry, each of these rich little desserts is truly satisfying. They're a welcome addition to a tray of assorted pastries and cookies.

■ Roll pastry into a 16x12-inch rectangle. Cut into fifteen 4-inch squares. Cover pastry with plastic wrap and set aside while preparing filling.

■ In a small mixing bowl beat cream cheese and egg yolk with an electric mixer till combined. Stir in the apricot or peach preserves. Spoon about *1 tablespoon* of the cream cheese mixture onto each pastry square. Moisten edges with a little water. Fold each pastry square in half diagonally, sealing edges well by pressing with the tines of a fork. Cut slits in top crust. Place on an ungreased baking sheet. Bake in a preheated 375° oven for 15 to 20 minutes, or till golden. Cool on a rack.

■ Meanwhile, in a small mixing bowl stir together the powdered sugar, vanilla, and enough milk to make an icing of drizzling consistency. Drizzle icing over warm turnovers.

Makes 15 turnovers

Per serving: 207 calories, 2 g protein, 24 g carbohydrate, 12 g total fat (4 g saturated), 21 mg cholesterol, 90 mg sodium, 32 mg potassium

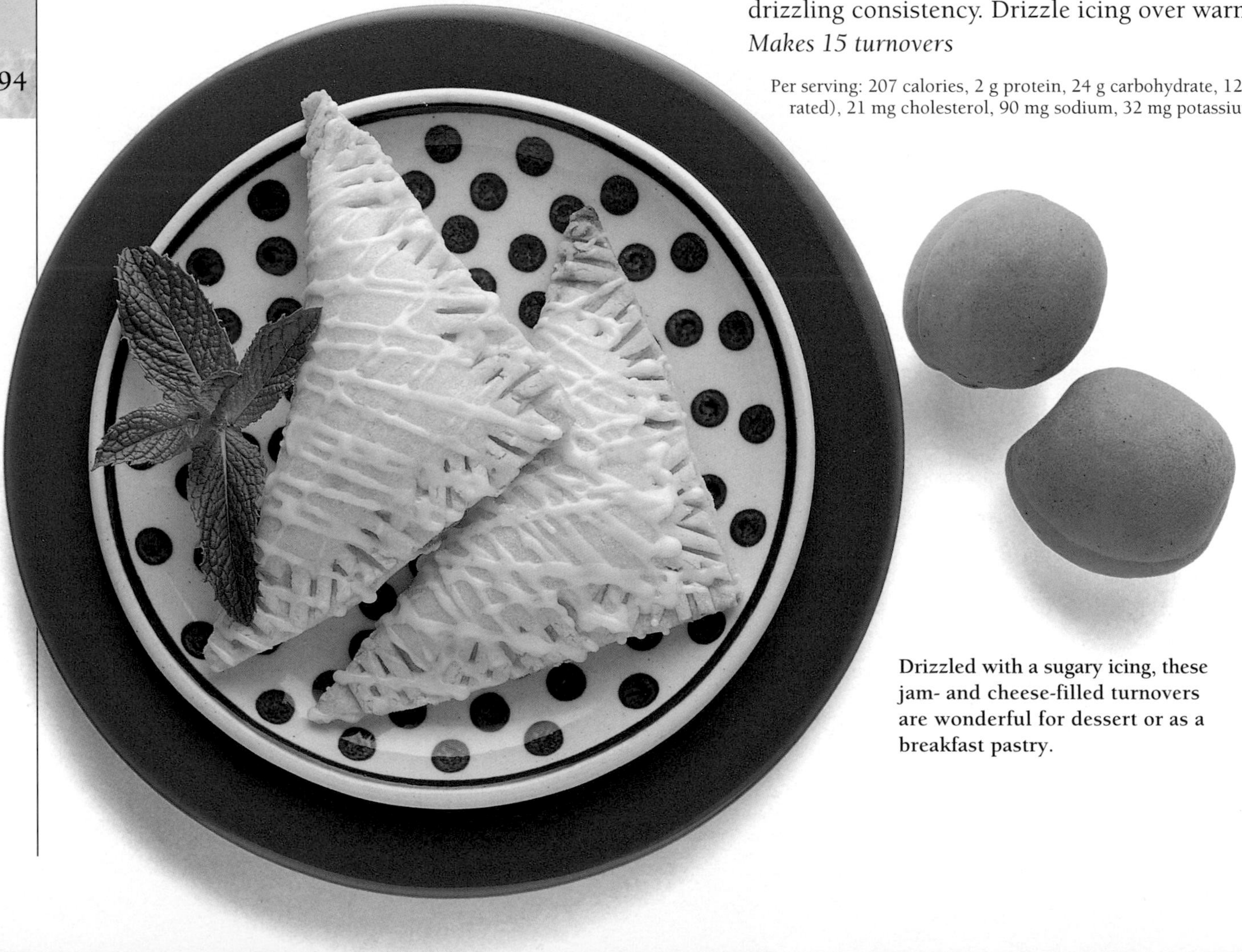

Drizzled with a sugary icing, these jam- and cheese-filled turnovers are wonderful for dessert or as a breakfast pastry.

Lamb & Feta Turnovers

Mini appetizer turnovers filled with Greek-inspired ingredients look pretty in a basket brimming with fresh herbs and cherry tomatoes.

STEPS AT A GLANCE	Page
MAKING DOUGH	8
MAKING TURNOVERS	82

Preparation Time: 50 minutes
Cooking Time: 5 minutes
Baking Time: 15 to 18 minutes

INGREDIENTS

6	OUNCES GROUND LAMB
1/2	CUP CRUMBLED FETA CHEESE
2	TABLESPOONS SLICED GREEN ONION
2	TABLESPOONS CHOPPED PITTED RIPE OLIVES
1/8	TEASPOON GROUND CINNAMON
1/8	TEASPOON GARLIC SALT
	PASTRY FOR DOUBLE-CRUST PIE (PAGE 14)
2	TEASPOONS MILK
2	TEASPOONS SESAME SEED

95

*F*eta cheese is traditionally made from sheeps' or goats' milk, then cured in brine. You can buy it in chunks, with or without the brine, or already crumbled in a package.

■ Cook lamb till no longer pink; drain. Stir in feta cheese, green onion, olives, cinnamon, and garlic salt. Set mixture aside.

■ Prepare pastry as directed. On a lightly floured surface, roll *half* of dough to slightly less than ⅛-inch thickness. Cut dough into rounds with a floured 3-inch round cutter. Spoon *1 rounded teaspoon* of the lamb mixture over half of each circle. Fold dough over lamb mixture. Using the tines of a fork, seal the edges. Repeat with remaining dough and lamb mixture. Cut slits in top crust. Place turnovers on an ungreased baking sheet. Brush with milk; sprinkle with sesame seed. Bake in a preheated 375° oven for 15 to 18 minutes, or till golden. Serve warm.

Makes about 24 turnovers

Per serving: 108 calories, 3 g protein, 7 g carbohydrate, 7 g total fat (2 g saturated), 7 mg cholesterol, 89 mg sodium, 31 mg potassium

Brunch Turnovers

Preparation Time: 45 minutes
Cooking Time: 3 minutes
Baking Time: 30 minutes

STEPS AT A GLANCE	Page
MAKING DOUGH	8
MAKING TURNOVERS	82

INGREDIENTS

	PASTRY FOR SINGLE-CRUST PIE (PAGE 14)
2	TABLESPOONS FINELY CHOPPED ONION
1	TABLESPOON MARGARINE OR BUTTER
1	BEATEN EGG
1	CUP SHREDDED CHEDDAR CHEESE
1	CUP FINELY CHOPPED FULLY COOKED HAM (5 OUNCES)
2	TEASPOONS SNIPPED FRESH DILL OR 1/2 TEASPOON DRIED DILL WEED
1/8	TEASPOON PEPPER
	DASH GARLIC POWDER
	MILK

*B*righten your morning with tasty packets of dill-seasoned meat and cheese. For a handy shape, fold each square in half to create a rectangular turnover.

■ Prepare pastry as directed, *except* roll the dough into a 15x10-inch rectangle. Cut into six 5-inch squares. Cover dough with plastic wrap and set aside.

■ In a small saucepan cook onion in hot margarine or butter till tender but not brown. In a medium mixing bowl combine egg, cheese, ham, dill, pepper, and garlic powder; stir in onion mixture. Spoon about *⅓ cup* of the filling onto each pastry square. Moisten edges of pastry with a little water. Fold each pastry square in half, sealing edges well by pressing with the tines of a fork. Place on an ungreased baking sheet. Prick tops. Brush lightly with milk.

■ Bake in a preheated 375° oven about 30 minutes, or till golden. Let stand for 10 minutes before serving.
Makes 6 servings

Per serving: 313 calories, 13 g protein, 20 g carbohydrate, 21 g total fat (7 g saturated), 63 mg cholesterol, 497 mg sodium, 130 mg potassium

96

Favorite breakfast ingredients — ham, cheese, and egg — go into these savory turnovers. Present them warm on a platter garnished with fruit and fresh dill sprigs.

Pastry Doughs

Steps for Making Cream Puff Pastry

HEAVY SAUCEPAN

BAKING SHEET

BASIC TOOLS FOR MAKING CREAM PUFF PASTRY

To prepare cream puff pastry, use a heavy saucepan and wooden spoon. Use a pastry bag and tip, or spoons, and forks for shaping, and a rack for cooling. A baking sheet is used for cooking puffs and éclairs.

WOODEN SPOON

TABLESPOONS

PASTRY BAG AND
1/2-INCH PLAIN TIP

COOLING RACK

FORK

Beyond pies and tarts lies a whole range of pastries made with specialized doughs: egg-rich cream puff pastry, flaky puff pastry, and tissue-thin phyllo. Each has its own special techniques and corresponding recipes, covered in this chapter. Cream puff pastry must be made from scratch. While puff pastry can be purchased frozen, the recipe on page 100 yields quick and easy results. Packaged phyllo dough is very good and widely available.

In the oven, moisture-rich cream puff dough inflates into crisp shells with tender interiors. Whether formed into large or small rounds or into elongated éclairs, they make perfect edible containers for pastry cream, whipped cream, mousse, or any number of savory fillings.

CREAM PUFF PASTRY

INGREDIENTS

1/2	CUP BUTTER
1	CUP WATER
1/4	TEASPOON SALT
1	CUP ALL-PURPOSE FLOUR
4	EGGS

■ Place butter in a medium saucepan. Add water and salt. Bring to boiling, stirring till butter melts. Add flour all at once, stirring vigorously. Cook and stir till mixture forms a ball that doesn't separate. Remove from heat; cool 10 minutes. Add eggs, one at a time, to flour mixture, beating with a wooden spoon after each addition for about 1 minute, or till smooth. Use as directed in recipe.

the ball of dough should be smooth and well combined

let mixture cool slightly before stirring in eggs so they don't curdle when added

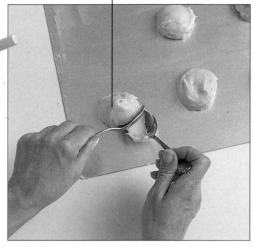

you can also use a rubber spatula to push the dough off the spoon

STEP 1 MAKING CREAM PUFF DOUGH

After the liquid comes to a boil, add flour all at once and stir vigorously until dough forms a ball that pulls away from the sides of the pan.

STEP 2 STIRRING IN THE EGGS

Add eggs, one at a time, beating after each addition for 1 to 2 minutes. The mixture will look lumpy at first, but after the last egg is beaten in, it will become thick, shiny, and silky as shown.

STEP 3 SHAPING CREAM PUFFS

Scoop up some dough with a tablespoon. Use another spoon to push off the dough in a mound onto the baking sheet. Leave 3 inches between the puffs for expansion.

fill the shells just before serving so they don't get soggy

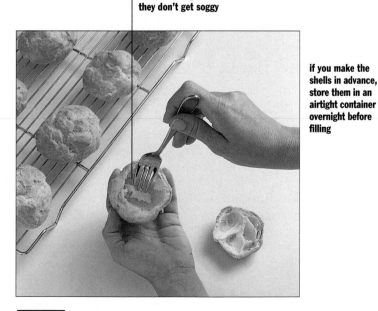

if you make the shells in advance, store them in an airtight container overnight before filling

to make smooth "fingers" of dough, lay the pastry bag almost flat to the baking sheet

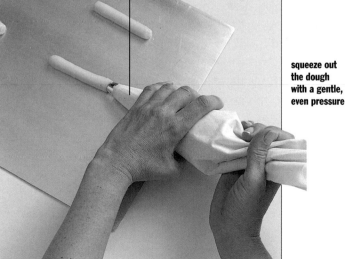

squeeze out the dough with a gentle, even pressure

STEP 4 HOLLOWING OUT CREAM PUFFS

Let the baked cream puffs cool on a rack. Slice off the tops (or cut in half). With a fork, gently scrape out any soft, moist dough. Work carefully so that you don't puncture the crust.

STEP 5 PIPING ÉCLAIRS

Fit a pastry bag with a ½-inch plain tip. Pipe strips of dough 3 inches apart onto a greased baking sheet. Cut off the dough with a knife at the tip for a neat finish.

Steps for Making Quick Puff Pastry

ROLLING PIN

LARGE BOWL

WOODEN SPOON

PASTRY SCRAPER

BASIC TOOLS FOR MAKING QUICK PUFF PASTRY

Use a bowl and wooden spoon to mix puff pastry dough, a metal dough scraper to help knead it, and a rolling pin to shape it.

100

PUFF PASTRY CONSISTS of hundreds of flaky layers, although the eye may only be able to pick out a fraction of that number. What creates these amazing layers? The secret is in the way fat is worked into the dough. Before it is shaped, the dough undergoes a series of rollings, foldings, and turns that results in alternating paper-thin sheets of dough and fat (in this case, butter). In the oven, the fat melts, creating empty spaces that are filled by air and steam. The air expands as it heats up, and the raw dough responds by rising as much as ten times its original height when fully baked.

If you have never made puff pastry, don't be intimidated by its demanding reputation. The process is not difficult at all, especially with this quick puff pastry recipe which uses a shortcut to incorporating butter and cuts down on the total number of turns.

Keep a few things in mind to head off any potential problems: To create flaky layers, use ice water and very cold butter, and chill the dough before shaping. Also, remember to give the dough a quarter turn between rolling and folding to work it in all directions. The recipe at right makes a double portion of dough; when a single portion is called for in a recipe, cut off half and freeze it for future use. It is always worthwhile to make enough pastry for two recipes.

QUICK PUFF PASTRY

INGREDIENTS

4	CUPS ALL-PURPOSE FLOUR
1	TEASPOON SALT
2	CUPS COLD BUTTER (1 POUND)
1-1/4	CUPS ICE WATER

■ In a large mixing bowl stir together flour and salt. Cut the cold butter into ½-inch-thick slices (not cubes). Add the butter slices to the flour mixture; toss till butter slices are coated with the flour mixture and are separated. Pour ice water over the flour mixture. Using a spoon, quickly mix (butter will remain in large pieces and flour will not be completely moistened).

■ Turn dough out onto a lightly floured surface. Knead dough 10 times by pressing and pushing dough together to form a rough-looking ball. Shape dough into a rectangle (dough still will have some dry-looking areas). Make the corners as square as possible. Slightly flatten dough.

■ Working on a well-floured surface, roll the dough into an 18x15-inch rectangle. Fold crosswise into thirds to form a 15x6-inch rectangle. Give dough a quarter turn, then fold crosswise into thirds to form a 5x6-inch rectangle and to create 9 layers. Repeat the rolling, folding, turning, and folding process once more, forming a 5x4-inch rectangle. Wrap dough with plastic wrap. Chill for 20 minutes. Repeat the rolling and folding process 2 more times. Before using, chill dough for 20 minutes more. To use dough in a recipe, cut in half crosswise with a sharp knife.

Makes two 1⅓-pound portions

use a large mixing bowl so there is room to toss the butter and flour together

do not toss with your hands, as your body heat will soften the butter pieces

a metal scraper will help gather the dough into a ball; also use it to remove any residue from your work surface before rolling

if necessary, sprinkle flour over the dough so the rolling pin doesn't stick

STEP 1 MIXING IN THE BUTTER

Combine the flour and salt. Cut the cold butter into ½-inch-thick slices and stir into the flour mixture. Toss until the butter slices are well coated with flour and separate from one another.

STEP 2 KNEADING THE DOUGH

Add the ice water and mix. The dough will look shaggy and the butter will still be in chunks. Turn out onto a lightly floured surface. Knead 10 times by pressing and pushing until the mixture forms a rough-textured ball.

STEP 3 ROLLING THE DOUGH

With lightly floured hands, shape the dough into a rough rectangle, flatten it slightly, and square off the corners. Roll the dough into an 18x15-inch rectangle.

101

generously flour the work surface so the dough doesn't adhere to it

to create full layers, fold so that the edges will meet all around

the dough will still look somewhat rough; it gets smoother with repeated rolling

always roll from the center out, stopping short of the edges so the layers are not pinched together

STEP 4 FOLDING INTO THIRDS

Make a letter fold: Working crosswise, fold one third of the dough to the center, then another third over it to form a 15x6-inch rectangle. Give the dough a quarter turn.

STEP 5 FOLDING AGAIN

Fold crosswise into thirds again to form a 5x6-inch rectangle. By folding, turning, and folding again, the dough is now in 9 layers.

STEP 6 ROLLING THE DOUGH AGAIN

Roll, fold, turn, and fold one more time. The dough will now be a 5x4-inch rectangle. Wrap with plastic wrap and chill for 20 minutes. Repeat the process 2 more times.

Steps for Shaping Puff Pastry

BASIC TOOLS FOR SHAPING PUFF PASTRY

BASIC TOOLS FOR SHAPING PUFF PASTRY
Use large and small knives, forks, and spoons to shape puff pastry. A cooling rack, icing spatula, bowl, and plastic bag are used for glazing.

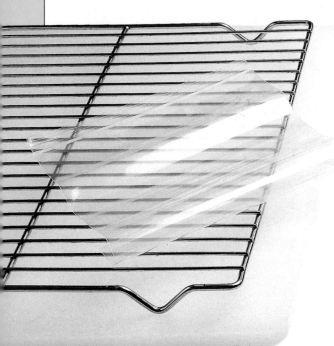

CUTTING BOARD AND
COOLING RACK

SLICING KNIFE

SMALL
PLASTIC BAG

PARING KNIFE

SPOON

BOWL

FORK

ICING SPATULA

R ICH, BUTTERY PUFF PASTRY has almost as many uses as it does crispy, paper-thin layers. Although deliciously fragile to bite into, it is surprisingly sturdy to work with and very versatile, whether rolled and sliced, separated into layers and filled, or shaped into a tartlike shell.

Palmiers and napoleons, two puff pastry classics, are demonstrated on these pages. Palmiers are melt-in-the-mouth cookies named after the palm leaves they are thought to resemble. They are formed out of a rectangle of dough that has been sprinkled with sugar or a cinnamon-sugar blend, then rolled tightly into pinwheels. Sliced and baked for cookies, they're superb with after-dinner coffee or tea. Or sandwich them with a rich filling as directed on page 114 and offer as a show-stopping dessert. Multilayered napoleons are filled with luscious pastry cream and fruit or sweet preserves. The smooth glaze on the topmost layer can be accented with a simple, easily accomplished pattern of chocolate chevrons.

A final tip: Always cut puff pastry straight down and with a very sharp knife. This keeps the layers separate so the dough will rise uniformly to its maximum height.

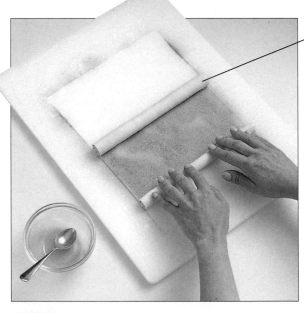

the finished pastry will look best if the dough is tightly rolled

STEP 1 SHAPING PALMIERS

Roll the puff pastry into a 14x10-inch rectangle. Sprinkle evenly with the sugar-cinnamon mixture. Lightly press into the dough with your fingertips. Roll up one short side like a jelly roll to the center of the rectangle. Roll the other short side the same way.

Cinnamon-sweetened palmiers and cream-filled napoleons are created from an easy puff pastry dough.

if the roll is too soft to cut, freeze it briefly to firm up

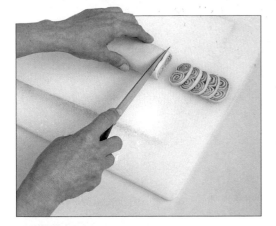

STEP 2 SLICING PALMIERS

Turn the pastry over so that the rolled sides touch the cutting board. With a sharp, thin-bladed knife, cut the roll crosswise into ¼-inch-thick slices. Don't press down as you cut, or the pieces will lose their shape and unroll.

103

as the pastry bakes, it naturally lifts into layers

be ready to pipe the chocolate immediately after icing, as the glaze hardens quickly

pipe chocolate from a plastic bag (see page 23)

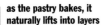

STEP 3 MAKING NAPOLEONS

Cut squares from rolled-out dough and bake until puffed and golden. Set on a rack to cool. With a fork, gently pry apart the baked pastry into 3 layers. Set aside for filling.

STEP 4 SPREADING THE GLAZE

Fill napoleons as directed in recipe. Spread the glaze over the top layer of pastry with a small frosting spatula, leaving a little of the pastry uncovered.

STEP 5 DECORATING NAPOLEONS

Pipe stripes of chocolate by sweeping back and forth across the glaze in one continuous motion. To create chevrons, draw the back of a knife gently one way through the lines, then reverse directions. Don't cut through the glaze.

Steps for Working with Phyllo Dough

CUTTING BOARD AND
BED SHEET

GLASS BOWL

SMALL PAN

WIDE PASTRY BRUSH

SLICING KNIFE

SPOON

BASIC TOOLS FOR WORKING WITH PHYLLO

Here's an unexpected kitchen tool: a
clean sheet for lifting strudel. A knife,
saucepan, bowl, pastry brush, and
spoon are no doubt on hand already.

A GENERATION AGO, translucent strudel dough, worked
and stretched until it covered the kitchen table, was
part of the repertoire of accomplished home bakers.
Today, few cooks attempt it, although some still do for
the satisfaction of making strudel completely from
scratch. Many of the recipes that may have formerly
called for homemade strudel pastry, like those in this
section, now substitute packaged phyllo dough.

Commercially prepared phyllo is readily available in
supermarket freezer cases. To use, defrost overnight in
the refrigerator or as directed on the package. Always
keep sheets of dough that are out on the counter lightly
covered with plastic wrap until you use them so they
won't dry out. For the same reason, use a generous
amount of melted butter or margarine between layers.

Whether shaped into bundles or triangles for appetizers, layered or rolled and filled with sweet or savory
ingredients, the uses for phyllo are seemingly endless.

buttering keeps
the phyllo moist
and holds the
layers together

STEP 1 **BRUSHING SHEET OF PHYLLO FOR STRUDEL**
Set a piece of thawed phyllo pastry on a clean, lightly
floured bed sheet (the sheet helps when rolling extra-long
strudel). With a wide pastry brush, cover the phyllo with
a generous amount of butter.

stagger the stacks so the seams are not all in one place

sometimes the dough needs coaxing with one hand to fall into a neat jelly-roll shape

spoon the filling about 1 inch in from one end of the strip to start the fold

STEP 2 **ADDING MORE STRUDEL LAYERS**

Cover the buttered phyllo with another layer. Butter one third of one long edge of the phyllo layers. Set a sheet of dough on this buttered strip so that it overlaps the first pair (you will create one long rectangle). Repeat process until you have a rectangle of phyllo layers that is approximately 18x40 inches.

STEP 3 **ROLLING UP STRUDEL**

Spoon a 4-inch-wide strip of filling along one short end of the stacked phyllo sheets, several inches in from one edge. To roll up the strudel, lift up the edge of the sheet nearest the filling to start the strudel rolling; continue lifting until dough is completely wrapped around filling.

STEP 4 **MAKING THE FLAG FOLD**

Cut stacked phyllo sheets lengthwise into 6 strips. Fold the end of a well-buttered strip over a spoonful of filling at a 45-degree angle. Fold up, then fold again at a 45-degree angle. Continue to the end of the strip, folding as for a flag.

105

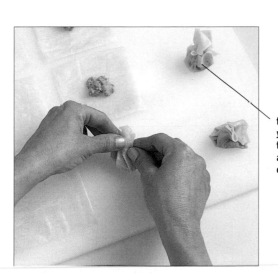

for decoration, you could tie the twisted area with a blanched green onion or chive

Layers of paper-thin phyllo make a crispy case for sweet and savory appetizers and strudels. Recipes appear on pages 110, 116, and 117.

STEP 5 **SHAPING A BEGGAR'S PURSE**

Place the filling in the center of a buttered square of stacked phyllo. Gather the square up around the filling like a sack; twist and pinch at the neck to seal.

Cream Puffs Praline

Preparation Time: 50 minutes
Baking Time: 30 minutes
Cooking Time: 7 minutes

INGREDIENTS

CREAM PUFF PASTRY (PAGE 98)

GLAZED PECANS

3/4	CUP PECAN HALVES
1/4	CUP GRANULATED SUGAR
1	TABLESPOON MARGARINE *OR* BUTTER
1/4	TEASPOON VANILLA
3	CUPS VANILLA ICE CREAM

PECAN SAUCE

3/4	CUP GRANULATED SUGAR
3/4	CUP PACKED BROWN SUGAR
1/2	CUP HALF-AND-HALF *OR* LIGHT CREAM
3	TABLESPOONS MARGARINE *OR* BUTTER
1/2	CUP CHOPPED TOASTED PECANS

106

These cream puffs can be filled with ice cream and stored in the freezer a day or two in advance, making them an excellent choice for entertaining. To serve, just spoon the warm sauce over the frozen puffs.

■ Prepare cream puff pastry as directed. Drop dough by heaping tablespoonfuls into 10 mounds, 3 inches apart, onto a lightly greased baking sheet. Bake in a preheated 400° oven about 30 minutes, or till golden brown. Remove puffs from pan. Cool on a rack.

■ Meanwhile, for glazed pecans, line a baking pan with foil. Grease foil with a little margarine or butter; set aside. In a heavy skillet combine pecan halves, sugar, margarine or butter, and vanilla. Cook over medium-high heat, shaking skillet occasionally, till sugar begins to melt. (Do not stir.) Reduce heat to low; cook till sugar is melted and golden brown, stirring frequently. Remove from heat. Pour into the prepared baking pan. Cool completely. Break into small pieces. Place ice cream in a chilled mixing bowl. Use a wooden spoon to stir ice cream to soften slightly. Stir in glazed pecans. Cover and freeze.

■ For pecan sauce, in a heavy saucepan combine granulated sugar, brown sugar, half-and-half or light cream, and margarine or butter. Cook over medium-high heat till boiling, stirring constantly. Reduce heat. Cook and stir for 5 minutes more, or till slightly thickened. Stir in pecans. Keep warm.

■ To assemble, cut off the top fourth of each cream puff. Remove any soft dough from inside. Spoon about ⅓ cup of the ice cream mixture into each cream puff. Replace tops. Drizzle each cream puff with warm pecan sauce.

Makes 10 servings

Per serving: 516 calories, 7 g protein, 57 g carbohydrate, 30 g total fat (13 g saturated), 132 mg cholesterol, 289 mg sodium, 247 mg potassium

STEPS FOR GLAZING PECANS

STEP 1 CARAMELIZING NUTS
Using a heavy skillet, cook the pecans in the sugar mixture until sugar is melted and golden brown. Handle carefully, as caramelized sugar is very hot. Pour into a foil-lined baking pan and let cool.

STEP 2 BREAKING PECANS
As the caramelized nuts cool they will harden. Break the sheet of nuts into small pieces by picking it up with your hands. Use immediately or store in an airtight container.

For your next dinner party, indulge your guests with ice cream–filled puffs topped with a rich pecan sauce.

Classic European pastries, such as napoleons, are often enjoyed as an afternoon pick-me-up with coffee or tea.

Chocolate-Raspberry Napoleons

Preparation Time: 45 minutes
Cooking Time: 10 minutes
Baking Time: 18 to 23 minutes

INGREDIENTS

1	PORTION QUICK PUFF PASTRY (PAGE 100) *OR* 1/2 OF A 17-1/4-OUNCE PACKAGE (1 SHEET) FROZEN PUFF PASTRY, THAWED

CHOCOLATE PASTRY CREAM

1/4	CUP SUGAR
2	TABLESPOONS ALL-PURPOSE FLOUR
1/8	TEASPOON SALT
1	CUP HALF-AND-HALF *OR* LIGHT CREAM
1	OUNCE SEMISWEET *OR* BITTER-SWEET CHOCOLATE, CHOPPED
2	SLIGHTLY BEATEN EGG YOLKS
1/2	TEASPOON VANILLA
1/4	CUP WHIPPING CREAM

GLAZE

2	CUPS SIFTED POWDERED SUGAR
1/4	TEASPOON VANILLA
2	TO 3 TABLESPOONS BOILING WATER
1/3	CUP SEEDLESS RASPBERRY PRESERVES
1-1/2	TABLESPOONS MELTED SEMI-SWEET CHOCOLATE

A traditional napoleon is filled with plain pastry cream; this version adds two more delicious flavors: chocolate and raspberry. To feather the icing as shown here, follow the method on page 103, but make finer lines of melted chocolate.

■ Line 2 baking sheets with parchment paper or plain brown paper; set aside. On a lightly floured surface, roll the dough into a 10-inch square. Using a sharp knife, trim off about ½ inch from all 4 sides to make a 9-inch square. (Or, if using purchased puff pastry, unfold sheet and trim edges to a 9-inch square.) Cut pastry into nine 3-inch squares. Transfer pastry squares to the prepared baking sheets; prick pastry. Bake in a preheated 425° oven for 18 to 23 minutes, or till golden. (Or bake according to package directions.) Carefully remove pastries from baking sheet. Cool on a rack.

■ Meanwhile, for chocolate pastry cream, in a heavy, medium saucepan stir together sugar, flour, and salt. Slowly stir in half-and-half or light cream; add chocolate. Cook and stir over medium heat till mixture is thickened and bubbly. Cook and stir for 1 minute more. Slowly stir about *half* of the hot mixture into beaten egg yolks. Return all to saucepan. Cook and stir for 2 minutes more. Remove from heat. Stir in vanilla. Transfer mixture to a bowl. Cover surface with plastic wrap and cool just till warm without stirring. In a small mixing bowl beat whipping cream till soft peaks form. Fold whipped cream into warm chocolate pastry cream.

■ For glaze, in a medium mixing bowl combine powdered sugar and vanilla. Stir in enough boiling water to make a glaze of spreading consistency; set aside. To assemble, use the tines of a fork to separate each pastry square horizontally into 3 layers. Spread about *1 teaspoon* of the raspberry preserves on each bottom layer. Spread about *1 ½ tablespoons* of the pastry cream over raspberry preserves. Top with middle pastry layers. Spread another *1 ½ tablespoons* of the pastry cream on each middle layer. Finally, top with remaining pastry layers. Spread glaze over top of napoleons, then drizzle with melted chocolate. Chill up to 1 hour.
Makes 9 servings

Per serving: 515 calories, 5 g protein, 62 g carbohydrate, 29 g total fat (17 g saturated), 120 mg cholesterol, 375 mg sodium, 110 mg potassium

109

STEPS FOR MAKING PASTRY CREAM

STEP 1 TEMPERING YOLKS

Beat the egg yolks in a heatproof bowl. Slowly stir in some of the hot chocolate mixture. This gently heats the yolks, or "tempers" them, so they won't curdle when added to the pastry cream.

STEP 2 COVERING SURFACE

To prevent a skin from forming on the cooked pastry cream as it cools, press plastic wrap directly onto the surface; let cool without stirring.

German Chocolate Strudel Braid

INGREDIENTS

STRUDEL BRAID

1	SLIGHTLY BEATEN EGG WHITE
1/2	CUP GROUND PECANS
1/2	CUP FLAKED COCONUT
1/2	OF A 4-OUNCE PACKAGE SWEET BAKING CHOCOLATE, CHOPPED
1/4	CUP SUGAR
2	TABLESPOONS MILK
1/4	TEASPOON VANILLA
6	SHEETS FROZEN PHYLLO DOUGH (ABOUT 18X12-INCH RECTANGLES), THAWED
1/4	CUP BUTTER, MELTED

TOPPING

1/3	CUP SUGAR
1/4	CUP WATER
2	TABLESPOONS HONEY
1/4	CUP TOASTED COCONUT
1/4	CUP TOASTED CHOPPED PECANS

*T*o toast the coconut and pecans for the topping, spread in separate pans and bake in a 350° oven for 5 to 10 minutes or until light golden brown.

■ For strudel braid, in a mixing bowl combine egg white, ground pecans, coconut, chocolate, sugar, milk, and vanilla; set filling aside. Unfold phyllo dough; remove 1 sheet. (Cover remaining phyllo with clear plastic wrap to prevent drying.) Place the sheet on a greased 17x14-inch baking sheet. Brush with some of the melted butter. Layer another sheet on the first, brushing top with butter. Repeat with remaining sheets and butter. Evenly trim edges of dough.

■ On both long sides, use scissors to make 4½-inch cuts from edge toward center, spacing the cuts 1 inch apart. Spoon the filling lengthwise down the center of the phyllo stack. Spread into a 3-inch-wide strip. Starting at one end, fold and slightly twist the phyllo strips at an angle over the filling. Tuck ends under. Brush top with remaining butter. Bake in a preheated 375° oven for 20 to 25 minutes, or till golden.

■ For topping, combine sugar, water, and honey. Bring to boiling. Reduce heat and simmer, uncovered, for 3 minutes. Transfer braid to a wire rack over a tray. Gradually spoon sugar mixture over braid, allowing it to soak in. Sprinkle with toasted coconut and pecans. Cool.

Makes 12 servings

Per serving: 205 calories, 2 g protein, 25 g carbohydrate, 12 g total fat (6 g saturated), 10 mg cholesterol, 93 mg sodium, 76 mg potassium

Preparation Time: 45 minutes
Baking Time: 20 to 25 minutes
Cooking Time: 3 minutes

STEPS FOR BRAIDING STRUDEL

STEP 1 CUTTING THE EDGES

With sharp kitchen scissors, make 4½-inch-long cuts from the edge to the center on each long side of the stacked phyllo sheets. Space the cuts 1 inch apart.

STEP 2 MAKING THE BRAID

Spoon the filling in a 3-inch-wide band down the center. To give the appearance of a braid, criss-cross the strips at an angle over the filling and across each other.

The time-honored combination of chocolate and coconut, made famous in German chocolate cake, inspired the filling for this superb pastry. Slice the braid with a sharp knife and serve with a pie server, or a strudel spatula as shown.

Chocolate Cannoli Éclairs

Drizzle chocolate over the éclairs with
a fork, or pipe from a plastic bag
as shown on page 23.

Preparation Time: 40 minutes
Baking Time: 30 to 35 minutes
Cooking Time: 2 minutes

INGREDIENTS

2	CUPS RICOTTA CHEESE
1/4	CUP SUGAR
4	TEASPOONS UNSWEETENED COCOA POWDER
1	TEASPOON VANILLA
1/3	CUP MINIATURE SEMISWEET CHOCOLATE PIECES *OR* CHOPPED SEMISWEET CHOCOLATE
3	TABLESPOONS CHOPPED CANDIED CHERRIES
	CREAM PUFF PASTRY (PAGE 98)
1/3	CUP MINIATURE SEMISWEET CHOCOLATE PIECES *OR* CHOPPED SEMISWEET CHOCOLATE
1	TABLESPOON SHORTENING
1	TEASPOON LIGHT CORN SYRUP
1/4	CUP CHOPPED PISTACHIO NUTS

*T*he luscious filling of ricotta, chocolate, and cherries is
similar to that used in cannoli, a well-known Italian
dessert. Here it fills traditional French éclairs.

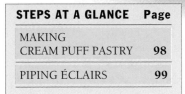

■ In a medium mixing bowl stir together ricotta cheese, sugar, cocoa powder, and
vanilla. Stir till smooth. Fold in ⅓ cup chocolate pieces or chopped chocolate and
the candied cherries. Cover and chill.

■ Prepare cream puff pastry as directed, *except* spoon dough into a decorating bag
fitted with a large plain round tip (about a ½-inch opening). Slowly pipe strips of
dough 3 inches apart onto a lightly greased cookie sheet, making 12 éclairs, each
about 4 inches long, 1¼ inches wide, and about ¾ inch high. Bake in a preheated
400° oven for 30 to 35 minutes, or till golden brown. Remove éclairs from baking
sheet. Cool on a rack.

■ Up to 1 hour before serving, horizontally cut off the tops of the éclairs. Remove
any soft dough from the insides. Fill éclairs with ricotta filling. Replace tops. Melt
⅓ cup chocolate pieces or chopped chocolate, shortening, and corn syrup over low
heat; drizzle or pipe over éclairs. Sprinkle with nuts. Chill.

Makes 12 éclairs

Per serving: 280 calories, 9 g protein, 23 g carbohydrate, 18 g total fat (9 g saturated), 104 mg cholesterol, 211 mg
sodium, 145 mg potassium

Italian Appetizer Puffs

Preparation Time: 45 minutes
Baking Time: 45 to 50 minutes
Cooking Time: 5 minutes

INGREDIENTS

ROASTED RED PEPPER SAUCE

2	RED SWEET PEPPERS
	DASH GROUND RED PEPPER
2	ANCHOVY FILLETS OR 1 TEASPOON ANCHOVY PASTE
1	TABLESPOON MARGARINE OR BUTTER

APPETIZER PUFFS

3/4	CUP WATER
6	TABLESPOONS BUTTER, CUT UP
1/2	TEASPOON DRIED OREGANO, CRUSHED
1/4	TEASPOON ONION SALT
1/4	TEASPOON DRY MUSTARD
3/4	CUP ALL-PURPOSE FLOUR
3	EGGS
1/4	CUP FINELY CHOPPED PEPPERONI
1/3	CUP THINLY SLICED PITTED RIPE OLIVES

*T*he distinctive roasted red pepper sauce used here would also be a good choice for serving with Zesty Italian Bites (page 91) in place of the spaghetti sauce, or toss it with fresh-cooked pasta and steamed vegetables.

■ For roasted red pepper sauce, quarter red sweet peppers. Remove stems, seeds, and membranes. Place peppers, cut side down, on a foil-lined baking sheet. Bake in a preheated 425° oven for 20 to 25 minutes, or till skin is darkened and blistered. Remove from baking sheet and place in a clean brown paper bag. Close bag tightly; cool 30 minutes. Remove skin from peppers; discard skin.

■ In a food processor bowl or blender container combine roasted peppers, ground red pepper, and anchovy fillets or anchovy paste. Cover and process or blend till smooth. Pour into a small saucepan; add margarine or butter. Heat and stir till margarine or butter melts. Bring to boiling. Reduce heat and simmer, uncovered, for 5 minutes. Keep warm.

■ Meanwhile, for appetizer puffs, in a medium saucepan combine water, butter, oregano, onion salt, and dry mustard. Bring to boiling. Add flour all at once, stirring vigorously. Cook and stir till mixture forms a ball that doesn't separate. Remove from heat and cool 10 minutes. Add eggs, one at a time, to butter mixture, beating with a wooden spoon after each addition about 1 minute, or till smooth. Stir in pepperoni.

■ Drop dough by well-rounded teaspoonfuls into 24 balls, 2 inches apart, onto a lightly greased large baking sheet. Bake in a preheated 400° oven about 25 minutes, or till golden and firm. Cool slightly on a rack. Split in half. Spoon a little red pepper sauce and a few olive slices in bottom half of each puff; replace tops. Serve warm.

Makes 24 appetizers

Per serving: 66 calories, 2 g protein, 3 g carbohydrate, 5 g total fat (2 g saturated), 36 mg cholesterol, 121 mg sodium, 35 mg potassium

Smaller than dessert-sized cream puffs, these appetizers are cut in half, rather than just being topped, before filling.

Strawberry Palmiers

You'll find many excuses to serve palmiers, which are small enough for a teatime snack, yet fancy enough for dessert.

Preparation Time: 30 minutes
Baking Time: 15 to 20 minutes
Cooking Time: 7 minutes

INGREDIENTS

PALMIERS

1	PORTION QUICK PUFF PASTRY (PAGE 100) *OR* 1/2 OF A 17-1/4-OUNCE PACKAGE (1 SHEET) FROZEN PUFF PASTRY, THAWED AND UNFOLDED
1/4	CUP SUGAR
1/2	TEASPOON GROUND CINNAMON

PASTRY CREAM AND GARNISH

1/2	CUP SUGAR
1/4	CUP ALL-PURPOSE FLOUR
1/4	TEASPOON SALT
2	CUPS HALF-AND-HALF *OR* LIGHT CREAM
4	SLIGHTLY BEATEN EGG YOLKS
1-1/2	TEASPOONS VANILLA
2	CUPS SLICED STRAWBERRIES
	WHOLE STRAWBERRIES

114

*T*hese palm-shaped pastries, known as palmiers, are layered with a vanilla-flavored pastry cream and fresh strawberries.

■ For palmiers, line 2 baking sheets with parchment paper or plain brown paper; set aside. On a lightly floured surface, roll the dough (or sheet of purchased pastry) into a 14x10-inch rectangle. Combine sugar and cinnamon; sprinkle over pastry rectangle. Lightly press sugar mixture into the dough. Roll the 2 short sides, jelly-roll style, to meet in the center. Turn pastry roll over and cut crosswise into ¼-inch-thick slices. If the roll is too soft to slice easily, chill it in freezer for a few minutes. Place slices 2 inches apart on the prepared baking sheets. Bake in a preheated 375° oven for 15 to 20 minutes, or till golden and crisp. Remove from baking sheet and cool on a rack.

■ For pastry cream, in a heavy medium saucepan stir together sugar, flour, and salt. Slowly stir in half-and-half or light cream. Cook and stir over medium heat till mixture is thickened and bubbly. Cook and stir 1 minute more. Gradually stir about *1 cup* of the hot mixture into beaten egg yolks. Return all to saucepan. Cook and stir 2 minutes more. Remove from heat. Stir in vanilla. Transfer pastry cream to a bowl. Cover surface with plastic wrap and cool just till warm without stirring. To assemble, spread about *2 tablespoons* of pastry cream over one side of *half* of the palmiers. Arrange sliced strawberries over pastry cream. Top each with another palmier. Garnish each palmier with a dollop of pastry cream and a whole berry.
Makes about 15 palmiers

Per serving: 393 calories, 5 g protein, 34 g carbohydrate, 27 g total fat (17 g saturated), 100 mg cholesterol, 431 mg sodium, 115 mg potassium

Shiitake Mushroom Appetizer

Shiitake mushrooms are brown mushrooms with large, floppy caps and a rich, meaty flavor. Once found only in specialty shops, they are now grown domestically and more widely sold. Look for them in specialty produce stores and some supermarkets.

■ On a lightly floured surface, roll the dough (or sheet of purchased pastry) into a 14½x9½-inch rectangle. Using a ruler and a very sharp knife, trim edges of pastry to form a 14x9-inch rectangle. Then cut the rectangle into one 14x6-inch rectangle and three 14x1-inch strips. Cut one of the 14x1-inch strips crosswise into two 4½-inch pieces. (There will be a 5-inch piece leftover.) Transfer the 14x6-inch rectangle to an ungreased baking sheet.

■ Combine the beaten egg yolk and water. Brush pastry rectangle with yolk mixture. Gently twist all the strips several times. Place them within ¼ inch of the edges of rectangle to form a rim around the edges, placing the 4½-inch strips on the ends. Moisten ends with yolk mixture, then lightly press together. Brush strips with yolk mixture. Prick center of pastry with a fork. Bake in a preheated 375° oven for 10 minutes.

■ Meanwhile, cook mushrooms and green onions in margarine or butter for 4 to 5 minutes, or till tender. Drain off any excess liquid; set aside. Stir cream cheese till smooth. Stir in sour cream, 1 egg yolk, fresh or dried rosemary, and pepper. Spread cream cheese mixture on partially baked pastry rectangle. Top with mushroom mixture. Return to oven and bake 10 to 12 minutes more, or till filling is set. Cut into strips or squares. If desired, garnish with fresh rosemary. Serve warm.

Makes 10 servings

Per serving: 346 calories, 5 g protein, 22 g carbohydrate, 27 g total fat (16 g saturated), 107 mg cholesterol, 364 mg sodium, 94 mg potassium

STEPS AT A GLANCE	Page
MAKING QUICK PUFF PASTRY	100

Preparation Time: 45 minutes
Cooking Time: 4 to 5 minutes
Baking Time: 20 to 22 minutes

INGREDIENTS

1	PORTION QUICK PUFF PASTRY (PAGE 100) *OR* 1/2 OF A 17-1/4-OUNCE PACKAGE (1 SHEET) FROZEN PUFF PASTRY, THAWED AND UNFOLDED
1	SLIGHTLY BEATEN EGG YOLK
1	TEASPOON WATER
3	CUPS SLICED SHIITAKE MUSH-ROOMS *OR* OTHER FRESH MUSH-ROOMS (8 OUNCES)
1/2	CUP CHOPPED GREEN ONIONS
2	TABLESPOONS MARGARINE *OR* BUTTER
1	3-OUNCE PACKAGE CREAM CHEESE, SOFTENED
1/2	CUP DAIRY SOUR CREAM
1	EGG YOLK
1	TEASPOON SNIPPED FRESH ROSE-MARY *OR* 1/4 TEASPOON DRIED ROSEMARY, CRUSHED
1/8	TEASPOON PEPPER
	FRESH ROSEMARY (OPTIONAL)

115

Thin strips of this savory puff pastry tart may be offered as an hors d'oeuvre or a stunning first course.

Apple & Dried Cherry Strudel

Traditional strudel dough is rolled and stretched paper-thin by hand. To save time, use frozen phyllo dough, which is completely prepared and easy to use. Thaw phyllo overnight in your refrigerator for best results when making strudel.

■ Pour enough boiling water over dried cherries to cover; let stand 20 minutes. Drain cherries. In a large mixing bowl combine brown sugar, flour, and cinnamon. Add apples and dried cherries; toss gently to mix. Set cherry mixture aside.

■ To assemble, cover a large surface with a floured bed sheet; unfold phyllo dough. Stack 2 layers of phyllo on the floured bed sheet, brushing between layers with some melted butter. Arrange another stack of 2 layers on the bed sheet, brushing between and overlapping stacks slightly. Add 3 or 4 more stacks, brushing and overlapping, forming a rectangle about 40x18 inches (stagger stacks so all seams are not down the middle). If necessary, trim to a 40x18-inch rectangle. Brush with melted butter.

■ Beginning 4 inches from one short side of the dough, spoon filling in a 4-inch-wide band across the dough. Using the bed sheet underneath as a guide, gently lift the 4-inch piece of dough and lay it over the filling. Slowly and evenly lift the bed sheet and roll up the dough and filling, jelly-roll style, into a tight roll. If necessary, cut excess dough from ends to within 1 inch of filling. Brush top with remaining butter; sprinkle with granulated sugar. Fold ends under to seal. Carefully transfer strudel roll to a lightly greased 17x14-inch baking sheet. Bake in a preheated 350° oven for 35 to 40 minutes, or till golden. Carefully remove strudel from pan. Cool on a rack.

Makes 12 to 16 servings

Per serving: 174 calories, 2 g protein, 31 g carbohydrate, 5 g total fat (4 g saturated), 14 mg cholesterol, 126 mg sodium, 83 mg potassium

116

Preparation Time: 50 minutes
Baking Time: 35 to 40 minutes

INGREDIENTS

1/2	CUP DRIED TART RED CHERRIES
1/2	CUP PACKED BROWN SUGAR
2	TABLESPOONS ALL-PURPOSE FLOUR
1/2	TEASPOON GROUND CINNAMON
3	CUPS THINLY SLICED PEELED COOKING APPLES (ABOUT 1 POUND)
10	TO 12 SHEETS FROZEN PHYLLO DOUGH (ABOUT 18X12-INCH RECTANGLES), THAWED
1/3	CUP BUTTER, MELTED
1	TABLESPOON GRANULATED SUGAR

STEPS AT A GLANCE	Page
WORKING WITH PHYLLO DOUGH	104

Sliced into wide strips on the diagonal and presented on a platter, this fruit-laden pastry is perfect as a breakfast pastry, afternoon snack, or make-ahead dessert for a crowd.

Curried Shrimp Phyllo Bites

If you use fresh cooked shrimp, sample the filling to make sure there's enough salt. Directions for both beggar's purse and flag fold shapes appear on page 105.

STEPS AT A GLANCE	Page
WORKING WITH PHYLLO DOUGH	**104**

■ In a small mixing bowl stir together yogurt, peanuts, chutney, curry powder, and gingerroot or ginger. Gently stir in shrimp.

■ Unfold phyllo; place 1 sheet of phyllo on a waxed paper–lined surface. Generously brush with some of the melted butter. Top with a second sheet; brush with more butter. Repeat with a third sheet. (Cover remaining phyllo with clear plastic wrap to prevent drying.) Using a sharp knife, cut the stack of phyllo crosswise into fourths, then lengthwise into thirds to make 12 squares. Using *half* of the filling, place about *2 teaspoons* in the center of each square. Form into a bundle or "beggar's purse" by bringing edges up to top of filling; twist together with a circular motion. Repeat with remaining phyllo dough, butter, and filling to make 24 bundles total. Or, cut and shape the phyllo using the flag fold. Place bundles or flags on an ungreased baking sheet. Bake in a preheated 375° oven for 18 to 20 minutes, or till golden.

Makes 24 appetizers

Per serving: 61 calories, 2 g protein, 5 g carbohydrate, 4 g total fat (2 g saturated), 14 mg cholesterol, 58 mg sodium, 42 mg potassium

Preparation Time: 35 minutes
Baking Time: 18 to 20 minutes

INGREDIENTS

1/3	CUP PLAIN YOGURT
1/3	CUP CHOPPED UNSALTED PEANUTS
3	TABLESPOONS SNIPPED CHUTNEY
1	TEASPOON CURRY POWDER
1/2	TEASPOON GRATED GINGERROOT *OR* 1/4 TEASPOON GROUND GINGER
1	4 1/2-OUNCE CAN TINY SHRIMP, DRAINED, *OR* 3/4 CUP FINELY CHOPPED COOKED SHRIMP
6	SHEETS FROZEN PHYLLO DOUGH (ABOUT 18X12-INCH RECTANGLES), THAWED
1/3	CUP BUTTER, MELTED

If you'd like to present these curried appetizers in Asian fashion, line your serving tray with ti leaves, available through most florists.

GLOSSARY

Refer to the following information when selecting many of the ingredients used in this book. Items are shown in photos clockwise from the upper left and are described in the text accordingly.

APPLES The best apple varieties for baking include mildly tart, red Jonathan; tangy, sweet, yellow-skinned Golden Delicious; and tart, green Granny Smith. Apples are available all year thanks to controlled storage. Choose firm, unblemished fruit; store in the refrigerator or in a cool, dark spot.

BERRIES Plush raspberries, round and juicy blueberries, tart cranberries, tangy-sweet blackberries, and brilliant red strawberries are favorites for pie fillings. Always select unbruised, slightly soft berries with deep color and inviting fragrance. Store unwashed and loosely covered in a single layer on a tray lined with paper towels in the refrigerator for a few days.

CHERRIES Sweet cherry varieties are best eaten out of hand. Most tart varieties are canned for pie fillings. Dried cherries boost the flavor of all kinds of baked goods. Store fresh cherries, covered, in the refrigerator up to 4 days. Tightly wrapped dried fruit lasts for months in the refrigerator or freezer.

CHOCOLATE The following chocolate types are commonly used in baking: *Milk chocolate* is a blend of at least 15 percent pure chocolate, extra cocoa butter, sugar, and milk solids. *Semisweet* contains at least 35 percent pure chocolate, extra cocoa butter, and sugar; *bittersweet chocolate* can be substituted although it is less sweet. *Unsweetened* is pure chocolate with no sugar or flavoring, while *cocoa powder is* pure chocolate with very little cocoa butter. Stored well wrapped in a cool, dry place, chocolate will keep up to 4 months.

CITRUS The juicy flesh and the aromatic oils stored in the colored peel of citrus fruits like lemons, limes, and oranges add fresh tart-sweet flavor to pastry. Key limes, the base for a famous chilled pie, are rarely found outside of Florida. Some specialty food stores stock Key lime juice. Select firm, heavy citrus fruit with healthy color; store 2 to 3 weeks in the refrigerator crisper.

COOKIES When crushed, mixed with melted margarine or butter, and pressed into a pan, packaged cookies make flavorful crusts for pies with chilled fillings. Spicy gingersnaps, rich chocolate wafers, classic vanilla wafers, and whole-grain graham crackers are found in most supermarkets.

COOKING FATS Margarine, butter, and vegetable shortening (in plain or butter flavor) are used in different phases of pastry making. Butter and shortening tenderize doughs and make them flaky. Margarine is often used in place of butter to moisten crumb crusts or enrich fillings. Use only regular margarine sticks, not diet, whipped, or liquid forms. Shortening is a vegetable oil–based fat manufactured to stay solid at room temperature. Butter and margarine will keep for a month, well wrapped in the refrigerator, or up to 6 months in the freezer. Store shortening at room temperature for up to 1 year.

FLOUR Wheat flour is the main structure-building ingredient in pastry. All-purpose flour has a medium protein content that makes it suitable for most baking uses. Whole-wheat flour is coarsely milled from the entire wheat kernel. Store all-purpose flour in an airtight container 10 to 15 months; store whole-grain flour up to 5 months. Or, refrigerate or freeze for longer storage.

GINGER The rhizome of a semitropical plant, ginger is marketed fresh, dried and ground into powder, and as crystallized or "candied" bits preserved in a syrup and coated in sugar. Select fresh gingerroots that are firm, not shriveled. Wrap in a paper towel and refrigerate for 2 to 3 weeks. Store ground and crystallized ginger in jars in a cool, dark place.

NECTARINES Like its relative the peach, a nectarine is a summer fruit that makes a delectable pie or pastry filling. Both freestone and cling (the fruit

APPLES

BERRIES

CHERRIES

CHOCOLATE

CITRUS FRUIT

COOKIES

COOKING FATS

FLOUR

GINGER

NECTARINES

118

NUTS

PEACHES

PEARS

PLUMS

RHUBARB

"clings" to the pit) varieties come to market. Choose unbruised, aromatic fruit without any tinges of green. Hold at room temperature, sealed in a paper bag, until fruit yields to gentle pressure. When ripe, refrigerate 3 to 5 days.

NUTS Pistachios, peanuts, pecans, walnuts, macadamias, and almonds add richness, texture, and flavor to pastry doughs and fillings. You'll find them in supermarkets packaged and in bulk in a number of forms, shelled or unshelled. Nuts are best used shortly after purchase; store in a cool, dry spot. Shelled nuts will keep longer if refrigerated or frozen airtight.

PEACHES Peaches may vary in the color of their skins (dark, reddish-brown to rich yellow to pink-tinged white) and flesh (yellow, white, or pale pink). Purchase well-shaped fruit, with obvious fragrance and no blemishes. A ripe peach is slightly soft; refrigerate when ripe for 3 to 5 days.

PEARS Of the many varieties of pears on the market, two are recommended for cooking. The elongated Bosc, with its russeted golden-brown skin and white flesh, and the narrow-necked, round-bottomed Bartlett (in either red or yellow). For baking, choose pears that are blemish-free and somewhat firm. Store ripe pears in the refrigerator 2 to 3 days.

PLUMS Fresh plums come to market from June through September in a variety of skin colors and sizes that can be used interchangeably in baking. Select firm (but not hard) plums that are plump and well shaped, with good color. A ripe plum will give slightly to pressure; refrigerate up to 5 days.

RHUBARB Called the pieplant because its slender stalks make a delicious pie filling, rhubarb is used like a fruit but is actually a vegetable. Only the stalks are edible; the leaves are toxic and are never eaten. Buy only crisp, firm, young stalks. If not used immediately, wrap and chill for up to 1 week.

SHIITAKE MUSHROOMS Asian shiitakes have floppy, deliciously meaty dark-brown caps and tough, thin stems that are usually trimmed off and discarded. Some recipes refer to them as black mushrooms. Fresh shiitakes are available in Asian markets or specialty produce stores. Select firm, fresh, plump mushrooms that aren't slimy or bruised. Store in the refrigerator, lightly wrapped in paper towels or in a paper bag, never in plastic, for up to 2 days.

SPICES For centuries, spices like cinnamon, cloves, mace, nutmeg, and ginger have added their distinctive character to baked goods. In the market, these spices are available dried. Spices lose flavor after about 6 months if ground and up to 2 years if whole. Store in airtight containers in a cool, dark, dry place.

SUGARS These sweeteners add flavor and color to doughs, fillings, and toppings. *Dark brown sugar* is a mixture of granulated sugar and molasses that adds rich, deep flavor. *Light brown sugar* has less molasses flavor than dark brown sugar. *Powdered sugar,* also called confectioners' sugar, is ground and mixed with a small amount of cornstarch to prevent caking. *Granulated sugar* is available in fine crystals (most common) and *superfine* (for frostings and meringues). It isn't necessary to use superfine sugar for the recipes in this book; they have been tested with granulated sugar. Store any type of sugar indefinitely in an airtight container.

TAPIOCA Tapioca starch thickens sauces, fruit fillings, and glazes, while the dried, pellet-sized balls of tapioca known as pearl tapioca are the base for custards and puddings. Look for tapioca starch in Latin American and Asian markets; pearl tapioca is commonly stocked by most supermarkets. Store indefinitely in a cool, dry place.

WHITE BAKING BAR Because it lacks pure chocolate, white baking bar (often called white chocolate) can't be considered a true chocolate product and shouldn't be substituted for chocolate in a recipe. It does contain cocoa butter, plus sugar, dry milk solids, and other flavorings. Store as you would chocolate, in a cool, dry place.

SHIITAKE MUSHROOMS

SPICES

SUGARS

TAPIOCA

WHITE BAKING BAR

119

INDEX

USING THE NUTRITION ANALYSIS

Keep track of your daily nutrition needs by using the information we provide at the end of each recipe. We've analyzed the nutritional content of each recipe serving for you. When a recipe gives an ingredient substitution, we used the first choice in the analysis. If it makes a range of servings (such as 4 to 6), we used the smaller number. Ingredients listed as optional weren't included in the calculations. Recipes for basic pastry do not include an analysis as they are only consumed as part of a recipe.